AF481231

EDITORS

Dr. Kanamala Arun Chand Roby, Pharm. D, MSc (PSY), PGDHHM, (PhD)
Assistant Professor
Department of Pharmacy Practice
Vignan Pharmacy College
Vadlamudi, Andhra Pradesh, India.

Dr. Kudipudi Harinadha Baba, M.Pharm, PhD, FIC, MBA (Hos Adm)
Professor and Principal
M.R. College of Pharmaceutical Sciences and Research,
Balisha West Bengal, India.

Mr. Yamarthi Venkateswara Rao, M.Pharm, (PhD)
Assistant Professor
Department of Pharmaceutical Analysis
Vignan Pharmacy College
Vadlamudi, Andhra Pradesh, India.

Foreword

The practice of pharmacy has evolved remarkably from a product-oriented profession to one that is predominantly patient-centred. As healthcare systems worldwide continue to emphasize the importance of medication safety, therapeutic efficacy, and interdisciplinary collaboration, the role of pharmacists has expanded significantly. Within this dynamic framework, **"Pharmacy Practice: Principles and Applications"** stands as a timely and comprehensive resource, designed to equip students, educators, and healthcare professionals with the knowledge and skills necessary to meet the ever-changing demands of modern pharmacy practice.

This textbook integrates foundational principles with practical applications, covering key areas such as clinical pharmacy services, drug therapy monitoring, patient counselling, pharmacovigilance, prescription handling, and interprofessional communication. The content aligns with current curricula for PharmD and B.Pharm programs, and also reflects global best practices in community and hospital pharmacy settings.

What distinguishes this work is its clarity of presentation, real-world relevance, and alignment with the evolving scope of the pharmacy profession.

The editors—**Dr. Kanamala Arun Chand Roby, Mr. Yamarthi Venkateswara Rao, and Dr. Kudipudi Harinadha Baba**—bring together a wealth of academic, clinical, and pedagogical experience. Their dedication to pharmacy education and patient care is evident throughout the pages of this work. They have succeeded in creating a text that is not only academically sound but also deeply practical, inspiring future pharmacists to uphold the highest standards of professional excellence.

It is my belief that this textbook will serve as a valuable companion to pharmacy students, educators, and practicing professionals alike. It will undoubtedly contribute to building a strong foundation in pharmacy practice and fostering a new generation of pharmacists committed to patient-centred care.

I congratulate the editors and contributors for their outstanding effort in bringing this important work to fruition.

[Dr. Kanamala Arun Chand Roby]

[Pharm. D, MSc (PSY), PGDHHM, (PhD)]

[Assistant Professor]

[Vignan Pharmacy College]

PREFACE

The profession of pharmacy has undergone a significant transformation—from a product-oriented discipline to a patient-centred clinical practice. In this changing healthcare environment, the role of pharmacists has expanded from dispensing medications to providing pharmaceutical care, ensuring optimal therapeutic outcomes, and promoting the rational use of medicines. This textbook, "Pharmacy Practice: Principles and Applications," is designed to bridge the gap between foundational pharmaceutical knowledge and real-world clinical application.

This book aims to serve as a comprehensive resource for undergraduate and postgraduate pharmacy students, educators, and practicing pharmacists. It provides a balanced blend of theoretical concepts and practical insights that are essential to modern pharmacy practice. The content has been meticulously structured to cover various facets of the discipline including medication history, prescription analysis, drug therapy monitoring, communication skills, pharmaceutical care planning, and the legal and ethical aspects of practice.

Each chapter has been written with clarity and precision, incorporating up-to-date guidelines, clinical scenarios, and relevant case studies to enhance understanding and application. Emphasis has been placed on the pharmacist's role in multidisciplinary healthcare teams, reflecting current global practices and standards.

We are confident that this textbook will not only serve as a strong academic foundation for students but also act as a practical guide for pharmacists in hospitals, community pharmacies, and other healthcare settings. The combined expertise and experience of the contributing authors ensure that the content is accurate, relevant, and reflective of contemporary practices in pharmacy.

We extend our sincere gratitude to our colleagues, reviewers, and students whose feedback and encouragement inspired the development of this work. We also acknowledge the constant support of our institution, Vignan Pharmacy College, for fostering academic excellence and innovation in pharmacy education.

We hope that **"Pharmacy Practice: Principles and Applications"** will contribute meaningfully to the professional growth of readers and inspire a commitment to excellence in pharmacy practice.

—The Editors

Dr. Kanamala Arun Chand Roby

Dr. Kudipudi Harinadha Baba

Mr. Yamarthi Venkateswara Rao

ACKNOWLEDGEMENT

We express our heartfelt gratitude to all those who contributed to the successful completion of this textbook, *"Pharmacy Practice: Principles and Applications."*

First and foremost, we thank the Management, Principal, and Faculty of Vignan Pharmacy College, Vadlamudi, for their constant encouragement, academic support, and infrastructure that facilitated the preparation of this work.

We sincerely acknowledge the invaluable guidance, insights, and inspiration provided by our mentors and colleagues in the **Department of Pharmacy Practice**, whose constructive feedback and collaborative spirit have significantly shaped the quality and depth of this book.

We are grateful to the practicing **clinical pharmacists, hospital staff, and healthcare professionals** whose real-world experiences and case-based discussions helped bridge the gap between theoretical principles and practical applications.

Our thanks also go to the students of **Pharm.D and B.Pharm**, whose curiosity and enthusiasm motivated us to compile and present the subject matter in a simplified and practical format.

Special appreciation is extended to our families for their patience, understanding, and unwavering support throughout this academic endeavour.

Finally, we thank the **publishers and editorial team** for their professionalism and commitment in bringing this work to publication.

We dedicate this textbook to the advancement of pharmacy education and to the students and professionals who strive to make a meaningful impact in patient care and healthcare delivery.

Dedicated with heartfelt gratitude to

God Almighty,

our beloved Parents, and

all Pharmacy students and professionals

who bloom with knowledge and compassion,

and work each day to enhance patient care.

PROLOGUE

Pharmacy Practice has evolved from a product-oriented profession to a patient-centred discipline that plays a vital role in the healthcare system. With the increasing complexity of pharmacotherapy, the pharmacist's role has expanded beyond the dispensing of medications to encompass clinical decision-making, patient counselling, drug therapy monitoring, and interprofessional collaboration. This transformation underscores the need for a comprehensive understanding of the principles and practical applications that govern modern pharmacy practice.

"Pharmacy Practice: Principles and Applications" is designed to bridge foundational knowledge with real-world clinical applications. The content of this textbook is structured to cater to the academic and practical needs of undergraduate and postgraduate pharmacy students, clinical pharmacists, and healthcare professionals involved in patient care. It covers a wide array of topics including the fundamentals of clinical pharmacy, pharmaceutical care, medication therapy management, interpretation of laboratory data, drug use evaluation, and the ethical and legal aspects of pharmacy practice.

The chapters are written with clarity, supported by recent guidelines and evidence-based practices, and are enhanced with case scenarios and illustrations to encourage active learning. Emphasis is placed on the development of critical thinking, communication skills, and the application of theoretical knowledge to clinical settings.

This textbook is the collaborative effort of educators and practicing professionals who are committed to advancing the role of the pharmacist in optimizing therapeutic outcomes. We hope this work will serve as a valuable resource for learners and practitioners alike, and contribute to the overall improvement of healthcare delivery.

We are deeply grateful to our mentors, colleagues, students, and institutions for their constant support and encouragement in bringing this book to fruition.

Editors

Dr. Kanamala Arun Chand Roby

Dr. Kudipudi Harinadha Baba

Mr. Yamarthi Venkateswara Rao

CONTENTS

HOSPITAL AND IT'S ORGANIZATION

Hospital is an organization and institution of public health and welfare. It provides healthcare facilities to ensure the wellbeing of people through specialized equipment handled by a group of specially trained individuals. Contrary to the common perception, a hospital not only takes care of sick people, it is also responsible for keeping a check on the wellbeing and maintaining health standards of the people in general. In order to keep them disease free and in good health, a hospital undertakes immunization, runs educational programs to spread information regarding personal and social hygienic practices.

According to WHO Expert Committee, 1963: The hospital is an integral part of a social and medical organization. The function of which is to provide for the population complete health care, both curative and preventive & whose outpatient services reach out to the family in its home environment; the hospital is also a center for the training of the health workers and for biosocial research.

Functions of Hospital

The major functions of a hospital are, 1. Treatment of patients 2. Prevention of diseases and 3. Education of public.

Classification:

1. Basing on objective

       a. General Hospital

       b. Special hospital

       c. Teaching cum research hospital

2. Basing administration, ownership, control or financial income

       a. Governmental or public

       b. Non- Government or private

       c. Semi Govt. Hospital

       d. Voluntary agency Hospital

3. Basing on length of stay

       a. Short –term or short stay hospital (stay less than 30 days)

       b. Long term or long stay hospital (stay more than 30 days)

4. Depending on type of medical staff:

       a. Closed – staff hospital

b. Open-staff hospital

5. Based on bed capacity(size)

    a. Small hospital (up to 100 beds)

    b. Medium hospital (more that 100 to less than 300 beds)

    c. Large hospital (more than 300 beds)

6. Basing on type of care:

    a. Primary care

    b. Secondary

    c. Tertiary care

7. Basing on system of medicine:

    a. Allopathic hospital

    b. Ayuredic Hospital

    c. Homeopathic hospital

    d. Unani Hospital

    e. Hospital of other system of medicine.

8. By teaching affiliation:

    a. Teaching hospital

    b. Non Teaching hospital.

9. Basing on regionality

    a. Regional

    b. District

    c. Upazila health complex

    d. Union Health & family welfare centers

    e. Community clinics

10. As per WHO classification:

    a. Regional Hospital

    b. Intermediate / District Hospital

    c. Rural Hospital

General Hospitals: General Hospital are meant to provide wide-range of various types of health care, but with limited capacity. They are for patients with various disease conditions for both sexes to all ages, medical, surgical, paediatric, obstetrics, eye and ear etc. Usually, general hospitals are devoid of super specialty medical care.

Special Hospitals: They limit their service to a particular condition, orthopaedics, maternity, paediatrics, geriatrics, oncology etc.

Teaching cum Research Hospital: College is attached for medial/ Nursing/ dental / pharmacy education. Main objective is to provide medical care, teaching and research is secondary.

Departments in the hospital:

Clinical Departments	Diagnostic & Support Departments	Administrative & Operational Departments
Emergency Department (ED / Casualty) Outpatient Department (OPD) Inpatient Department (Wards) Intensive Care Unit (ICU) Surgery / Operating Theatre (OT) Anaesthesiology Obstetrics and Gynaecology (OB-GYN) Paediatrics Internal Medicine Orthopaedics Cardiology Neurology Oncology Nephrology Gastroenterology Dermatology Psychiatry ENT (Ear, Nose, Throat) Urology Pulmonology / Respiratory Medicine	Radiology / Imaging (X-ray, CT, MRI, Ultrasound) Pathology / Clinical Laboratory Pharmacy Blood Bank / Transfusion Services Physiotherapy / Rehabilitation Nutrition and Dietetics	Medical Records Department (MRD) Billing and Accounts Human Resources Biomedical Engineering Information Technology (IT) Housekeeping and Maintenance Security and Transport Laundry Services Central Sterile Supply Department (CSSD)

Organization Structure of a hospital:

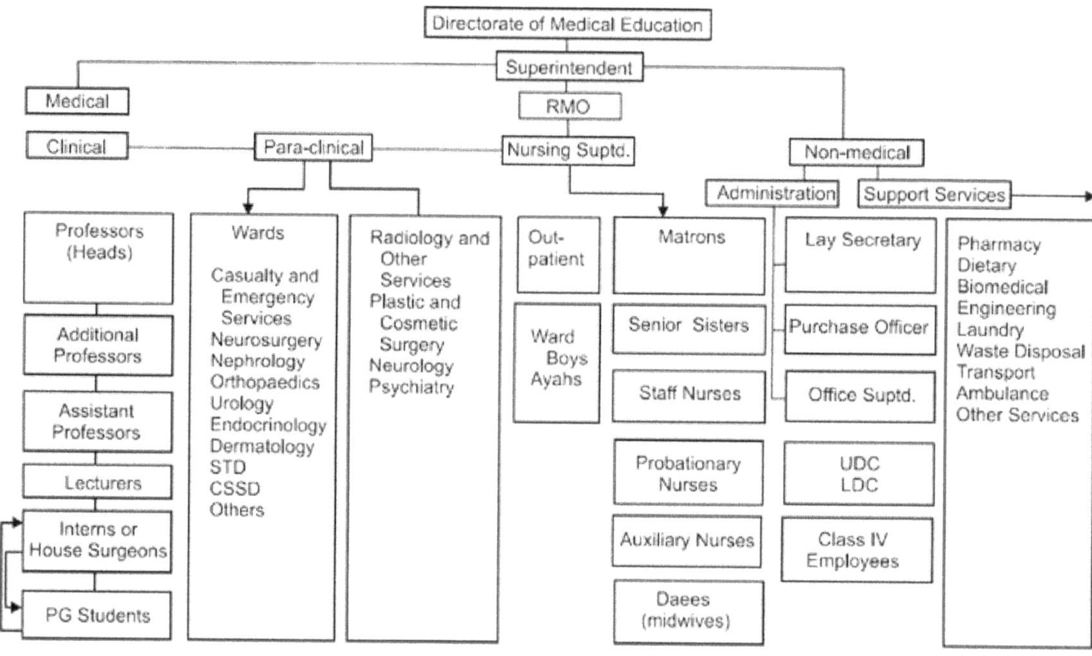

Note: **CSSD** Central Sterile Services Department; **LDC** Lower Division Clerk; **PG** Postgraduate; **RMO** Resident Medical Officer; **STD** Sexually Transmitted Disease; **UDC** Upper Division Clerk.

1. Directorate of Medical Education

Overall administrative authority, Coordinates with teaching hospitals and ensures quality standards.

Approves curriculum, staffing, and infrastructure planning.

2. Superintendent

Directly oversees the hospital operations, nurses smooth day-to-day functioning of clinical and non-clinical departments, Liaison between hospital departments and government health authorities.

Resident Medical Officer (RMO)

Nursing Superintendent

3. Divisions Under Superintendent

A. Medical Division

1. Clinical

Professors (Heads)

Additional Professors

Assistant Professors

Lecturers

Interns or House Surgeons

Postgraduate (PG) Students

2. **Para-clinical**

   Wards:

   Casualty and Emergency Services

   Neurosurgery

   Nephrology

   Orthopaedics

   Urology

   Endocrinology

   Dermatology

   STD (Sexually Transmitted Diseases)

   CSSD (Central Sterile Services Department)

   Others

   Radiology and Other Services:

   Plastic and Cosmetic Surgery

   Neurology

   Psychiatry

   Wards (Medical & Surgical Specialties)

Casualty/Emergency: Immediate care for trauma, poisoning, cardiac emergencies.

Neurosurgery, Nephrology, Urology, etc.: Specialized inpatient and outpatient services.

CSSD: Responsible for sterilization of surgical instruments and supplies.

STD Clinic: Diagnosis, treatment, and prevention of sexually transmitted infections.

▸ **Radiology and Other Services**

Imaging and diagnostic support (X-ray, MRI, CT scan).

Plastic surgery, psychiatry, neurology services for comprehensive care.

B. Nursing Division

Matrons

Senior Sisters

Staff Nurses

Probationary Nurses

Auxiliary Nurses

Dais (Midwives)

Out-patient Staff (Ward Boys, Ayahs)

C. Non-medical Division

1. **Administration:**

   Lay Secretary

   Purchase Officer

   Office Superintendent

   UDC (Upper Division Clerk)

   LDC (Lower Division Clerk)

   Class IV Employees

2. **Support Services:**

   Pharmacy

   Dietary

   Biomedical Engineering

   Laundry

   Waste Disposal

   Transport

   Ambulance

   Other Services

Medical Staff in a Hospital and Their Functions

1. Medical Superintendent / Chief Medical Officer

Overall, in-charge of medical services in the hospital.

Functions:

Supervises all clinical and medical operations.

Coordinates between departments.

Ensures compliance with medical standards and policies.

Handles crisis or emergency situations.

2. Resident Medical Officer (RMO)

Manages in-house medical activities on a day-to-day basis.

Functions:

Monitors patient admissions and discharges.

Provides immediate care in emergencies.

Coordinates with doctors for patient care.

Maintains patient records.

3. Consultants / Specialists

Senior doctors specialized in a particular field (e.g., Cardiologist, Neurologist).

Functions:

Diagnose and treat complex cases.

Perform surgeries or specialized procedures.

Mentor and supervise junior doctors and interns.

Contribute to clinical audits and teaching (in teaching hospitals).

4. Medical Officers / General Physicians

General practitioners providing primary care.

Functions:

Initial diagnosis and treatment.

Routine ward rounds and follow-ups.

Assist specialists in patient care.

Write medical reports and prescriptions.

5. House Surgeons / Interns

Fresh medical graduates under supervised training.

Functions:

Assist senior doctors during rounds and procedures.

Perform basic clinical duties like history taking, dressing, IV lines.

Learn practical aspects of patient management.

Participate in emergency duties.

6. Postgraduate Students / Residents

Medical graduates pursuing specialization.

Functions:

Manage patients under the guidance of consultants.

Perform minor procedures and assist in major ones.

Conduct clinical research.

Teach interns or juniors.

7. Surgeons

Perform operative procedures.

Functions:

Evaluate surgical candidates.

Perform planned or emergency surgeries.

Manage pre-operative and post-operative care.

Train junior surgical staff.

8. Anaesthesiologists

Provide anaesthesia during surgeries.

Functions:

Assess patients before surgery.

Administer and monitor anaesthesia.

Manage pain control post-surgery.

Respond to resuscitation and critical care.

9. Radiologists

Specialists in medical imaging.

Functions:

Interpret X-rays, CT, MRI, ultrasound scans.

Guide interventional procedures (e.g., biopsies).

Support diagnosis and treatment planning.

10. Pathologists

Experts in diagnosing diseases through lab testing.

Functions:

Examine blood, tissue, and body fluids.

Provide diagnostic reports.

Collaborate in cancer and infection diagnosis.

11. Emergency Physicians

Immediate care providers in emergencies.

Functions:

Stabilize trauma and critically ill patients.

Make rapid decisions on care.

Coordinate with surgical or ICU teams.

12. Paediatricians

Child health specialists.

Functions:

Provide preventive and curative care for children.

Monitor growth and development.

Immunizations and nutritional advice.

13. Obstetricians & Gynaecologists

Specialists in women's reproductive health.

Functions:

Manage pregnancy, labour, and delivery.

Treat gynaecological disorders.

Conduct surgeries like hysterectomy, C-section.

14. Psychiatrists

Manage mental health conditions.

Functions:

Diagnose and treat psychiatric disorders.

Prescribe medications and therapy.

Support counselling and de-addiction programs.

15. Dentists (in hospitals with dental wings)

Functions:

Perform dental checkups and treatments.

Conduct oral surgeries.

Educate on oral hygiene.

Hospitals are the cornerstones of the healthcare system, designed to provide comprehensive medical care, including prevention, diagnosis, treatment, and rehabilitation. The organization of a hospital plays a crucial role in ensuring that these services are delivered efficiently and effectively.

A well-organized hospital features a clearly defined hierarchy, distinct departments, and interdisciplinary coordination that together enable the seamless flow of patients, information, and resources. From administrative leadership to clinical departments and support services, each unit functions in harmony to fulfil the hospital's goals of patient care, education, and research.

The proper organization of a hospital enhances:

Quality of care

Operational efficiency

Patient safety

And staff accountability

Ultimately, an efficiently organized hospital is better equipped to meet the ever-growing healthcare needs of society, adapting to challenges while maintaining high standards of care.

HOSPITAL PHARMACY AND IT'S ORGANISATION

Hospital Pharmacy

Hospital pharmacy is a specialized field within pharmacy practice those functions as an integral component of hospital healthcare systems. It involves the preparation, compounding, dispensing, storage, and management of medications, alongside the provision of clinical services. The primary objective is to ensure the safe, effective, and rational use of medicines in patient care.

Functions of a Hospital Pharmacy

Hospital pharmacies play a vital role in the delivery of healthcare services by ensuring optimal medication use. The main functions include:

1. **Dispensing Medications**

   Dispensing prescribed drugs to inpatients and outpatients while ensuring accuracy in dosage, labelling, and administration.

2. **Medication Inventory Management**

   Maintaining adequate stocks of essential medications, monitoring expiry dates, and ensuring uninterrupted drug availability.

3. **Clinical Pharmacy Services**

   Collaborating with physicians and other healthcare professionals to review medication regimens, monitor therapeutic outcomes, and prevent adverse drug reactions and medication errors.

4. **Sterile Preparation and Compounding**

   Preparing sterile injectable medications, total parenteral nutrition (TPN), and other compounded formulations under aseptic conditions.

5. **Patient Counselling and Education**

   Providing patients with information on proper medication usage, potential side effects, and adherence to therapy.

6. **Drug Safety and Pharmacovigilance**

   Monitoring and documenting adverse drug reactions (ADRs) and ensuring adherence to safety guidelines and regulatory standards.

7. **Support for Research and Clinical Trials**

   Assisting in investigational drug studies, maintaining documentation, and ensuring compliance with clinical trial protocols.

8. **Policy Formulation and Quality Control**

Participating in the development of hospital drug policies, standard treatment guidelines, and implementing quality assurance measures.

9. **Interdisciplinary Collaboration**

Working alongside doctors, nurses, and other healthcare providers to contribute to comprehensive patient care and therapeutic planning.

Organizational Structure of a Hospital Pharmacy

The structure of a hospital pharmacy is typically hierarchical, ensuring clarity in responsibilities and effective functioning. The general organization includes:

1. **Director of Pharmacy / Chief Pharmacist**

Responsible for overall administration, policy development, budgeting, and strategic planning of pharmacy services.

2. **Pharmacy Managers / Department Supervisors**

Oversee specific departments such as inpatient services, outpatient dispensing, or clinical pharmacy. They supervise daily operations and enforce regulatory compliance.

3. **Clinical Pharmacists**

Engage in direct patient care activities, participate in ward rounds, evaluate drug therapy regimens, and provide clinical consultations.

4. **Staff Pharmacists**

Handle routine dispensing, verify prescriptions, provide drug information, and assist in patient education.

5. **Pharmacy Technicians**

Support pharmacists by preparing medications, managing inventory, compounding non-sterile products, and maintaining records.

6. **Support and Administrative Personnel**

Includes pharmacy assistants who handle clerical tasks and stock replenishment, as well as administrative staff who manage billing, insurance claims, and documentation.

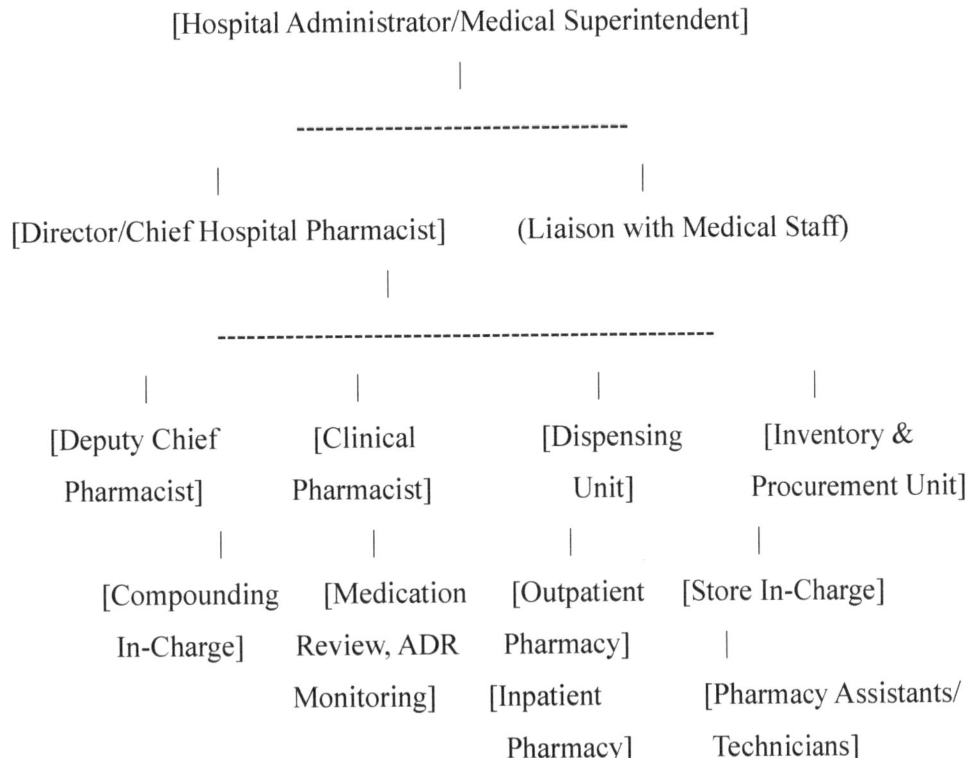

Location, Layout, and Staff Requirements of a Hospital Pharmacy:

1. Location of Hospital Pharmacy

The hospital pharmacy should be **strategically located** to ensure accessibility and efficiency:

- **Proximity to patient care areas:** Ideally near wards, emergency, and outpatient departments to ensure timely dispensing.
- **Central location:** Allows for easy coordination with other departments (nursing, medical, stores).
- **Separate entry/exit:** For receiving supplies and reducing congestion.
- **Secure and controlled area:** To limit access only to authorized personnel.

2. Layout of Hospital Pharmacy

An ideal hospital pharmacy layout ensures **efficient workflow, safety, and regulatory compliance**. The layout includes:

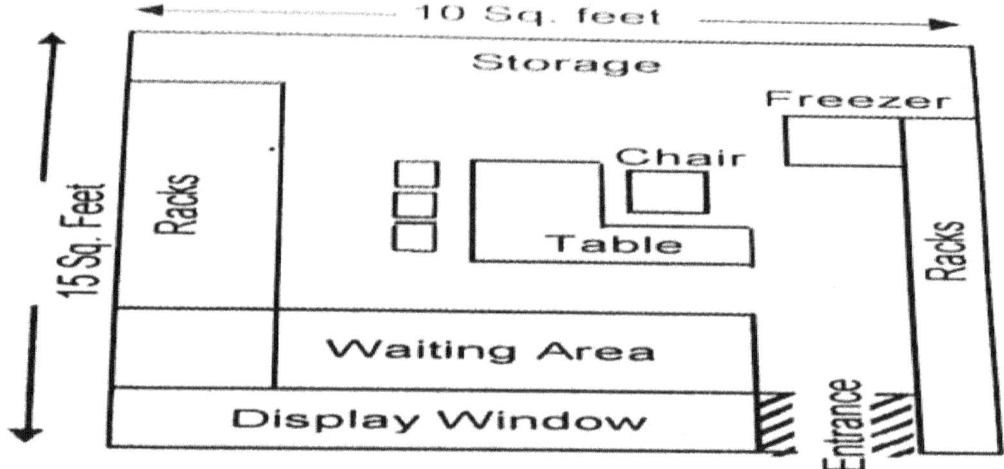

Retail drug store design

a) Dispensing Area

- For outpatient and inpatient medication distribution.
- Equipped with dispensing counters and medication bins.
- Sufficient space for queue management.

b) Drug Storage Area

- Segregated zones for:
    - **Controlled substances**
    - **Cold chain products** (vaccines, insulin)
    - **Hazardous drugs**
    - **Bulk storage** and **fast-moving items**
- Proper **ventilation, lighting**, and **temperature control**.

c) Compounding and Preparation Area

- **Aseptic room** for sterile preparations (IV fluids, parenterals).
- **Non-sterile compounding area** for powders, ointments, etc.
- Laminar airflow units and clean benches where applicable.

d) Office and Record Room

- For administrative work, documentation, inventory records, and communication.

e) Waiting Area

- Especially for OPD pharmacies.
- Should be comfortable, with seating and informational displays.

f) Waste Disposal Area

- For expired drugs, cytotoxic waste, and sharps.
- Should comply with **Biomedical Waste Management Rules**.

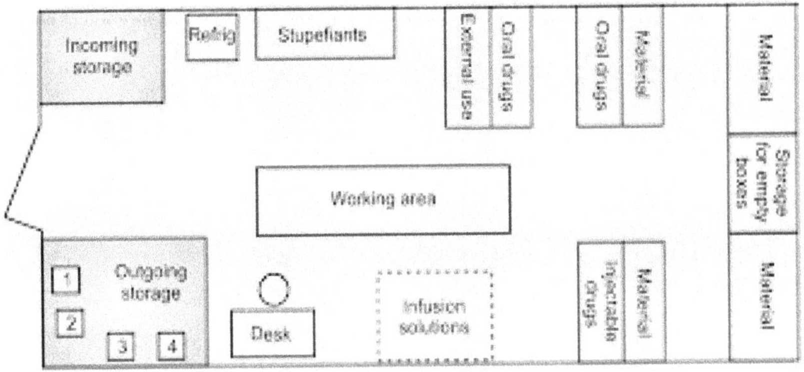

Layout of Hospital Pharmacy

3. Staff Requirements of Hospital Pharmacy

Staffing depends on the **size and function** of the hospital (primary, secondary, tertiary care).

Common positions include:

a) Chief Pharmacist / Pharmacy Superintendent

- Overall supervision.
- Policy formulation and compliance.
- Reporting to the hospital administration.

b) Pharmacists

- Responsible for dispensing, inventory management, patient counselling.
- Should hold a diploma or degree in pharmacy and be registered.

c) Clinical Pharmacists

- Work in coordination with medical staff.
- Conduct drug therapy monitoring, medication reconciliation, and patient education.

d) Pharmacy Technicians / Assistants

- Help with labelling, stocking, and record maintenance.

e) Support Staff

- Cleaners, clerks, data entry operators, and messengers.

Typical Staff Pattern (For a 100-bedded hospital):

Staff Category	Number (Approx.)
Chief Pharmacist	1
Senior Pharmacists	2–3
Junior Pharmacists	3–5
Technicians/Assistants	2–4

| Support Staff | 2–3 |

Staffing ratios and layout may vary based on country-specific regulations, NABH/JCI guidelines, and hospital accreditation standards.

Responsibilities and functions of hospital pharmacists.

Responsibilities

- **Dispensing medications** – Ensuring patients receive the correct dosage and instructions for their prescribed drugs.
- **Monitoring drug therapy** – Tracking the effectiveness of treatments and adjusting medications as needed.
- **Educating patients and healthcare professionals** – Providing guidance on drug interactions, side effects, and proper usage.
- **Ensuring medication safety** – Preventing adverse drug reactions and medication errors.
- **Managing hospital drug supply** – Procuring, storing, and maintaining stock of essential medications.
- **Collaborating with medical teams** – Working alongside doctors and nurses to optimize patient treatment plans.
- **Conducting research** – Developing and testing new drug therapies to improve patient outcomes.

Functions

- **Clinical pharmacy services** – Assessing individual patients' medication needs and providing personalized pharmaceutical care.
- **Formulary management** – Selecting and standardizing medications used within the hospital.
- **Sterile compounding** – Preparing specialized medications such as intravenous drugs and chemotherapy agents.
- **Pharmacovigilance** – Detecting and reporting adverse drug reactions to ensure medication safety.
- **Regulatory compliance** – Ensuring adherence to healthcare laws and standards related to pharmaceuticals.
- **Providing drug information** – Acting as a resource for healthcare professionals regarding medication options and best practices.

ADVERSE DRUG REACTION

The World Health Organization defines as adverse drug reaction as "Any noxious and unintended effect of drug which occurs at doses normally used in man for the prophylaxis diagnosis or therapy of disease or for the modification of physiological functions.

Any untoward medical occurrence that may present during treatment with a pharmaceutical product but which does not necessarily have a causal relationship with this treatment.

Adverse Drug Reaction (ADR): Any noxious change which is suspected to be due to a drug, occurs at doses normally used in man, requires treatment or decrease in dose or indicates caution in future use of the same drug. Therefore, an adverse drug reaction is an adverse event with a causal link to a drug.

Classification of ADRs.... Depending

Onset of event: Acute (<60 minutes), Sub-acute (1-24 hrs) and Latent (>2 days)

Type of reaction: Type A (Augmented), B (Bizarre), C (Chemical),D (Delayed), E (Exit), F (Familial), G (Genotoxicity), H (Hypersensitivity), U (Un classified)

Severity: Minor, Moderate, Severe, Lethal ADRs

Others: Side effects, Secondary effects, Toxic effects, Intolerance, Idiosyncrasy, Drug allergy, Photosensitivity, Drug Dependence, Drug Withdrawal Reactions, Teratogenicity, Mutagenicity, Carcinogenicity, Drug induced disease (Iatrogenic)

Classification of ADRs

Type A (Augmented)

Type B (Bizarre)

Type C (Chemical)

Type D (Delayed)

Type E (Exit/End of treatment)

Type F (Familial)

Type G (Genotoxicity)

Type H (Hypersensitivity)

Type U (Un classified)

> **Type A (Augmented)** reactions which can be predicted from the known pharmacology of the drug Dose dependent, can be alleviated by a dose reduction E.g. Anticoagulants, Bleeding, Beta blockers, Bradycardia, Nitrates, Headache, Prazosin Postural hypotension.

<u>**Type B (Bizarre)**</u> reactions Cannot be predicted from the pharmacology of the drug Not dose dependent, Host dependent factors important in predisposition E.g. Penicillin Anaphylaxis, Anticonvulsant Hypersensitivity

<u>**Type C (Chemical)**</u> reactions biological characteristics can be predicted from the chemical structure of the drug/metabolite E.g. Paracetamol Hepatotoxicity

<u>**Type D (Delayed)**</u> reactions Occur after many years of treatment. Can be due to accumulation. E.g. Chemotherapy Secondary Tumours Phenytoin during pregnancy Teratogenic effects Antipsychotics Tardive dyskinesia Analgesics Nephropathy

<u>**Type E (End**</u> of treatment) reactions Occur on withdrawal especially when drug is stopped abruptly E.g.Phenytoin withdrawal Seizures, Steroid withdrawal Adrenocortical insufficiency

Type F (Failure of treatment): Common to all, Often caused by drug interactions

Classification of ADRs…. Depending on Severity

Minor ADRs: No therapy, antidote or prolongation of hospitalization is required.

Moderate ADRs: Requires change in drug therapy, specific treatment or prolongs hospital stay by atleast 1 day.

Severe ADRs: Potentially life threatening, causes permanent damage or requires intensive medical treatment.

Lethal: Directly or indirectly contributes to death of the patient.

DoTS Classification of ADRs:

A. Dose

B. Timing

C. Susceptibility

DoTS Classification of ADRs: A. Dose:

Below Therapeutic dose – Eg: Anaphylaxis with penicillin

In therapeutic dose range – Eg: Nausea with morphine

At high dose – Eg: Hepatotoxicity with paracetamol

DoTS Classification of ADRs: B. Timing:

With the first dose – Anaphylaxis with penicillin

Early stages of treatment – Hyponatremia with diuretics

On stopping treatment – Benzodiazepine withdrawal syndrome

Significantly delayed – clear cell carcinoma with DES

DoTS Classification of ADRs: C. Susceptibility:

Elderly age

Gender

Polypharmacy

Genetic Predispostion

Disease altering pharmacokinetics

Adherence problems

PREDISPOSING FACTORS FOR ADR

1. Polypharmacy

2. Multiple and inter-current diseases

3. Age

4. Drug characteristics

5. Gender

6. Race and genetic factors

Polypharmacy: Multiple drug therapy – more prone to develop ADR

Either due to interaction mechanism or by synergistic effect

Multiple and inter-current diseases:

Multiple diseases are at increased risk of developing an ADR

Patient with renal and hepatic diseases are also at high risk

Eg: Patient with decreased renal function treated with normal dose of aminoglycosides is at risk of developing nephrotoxicity until dose adjustment

Age: Elderly and paediatric patients are more vulnerable to ADRs

Elderly patient are more susceptible due to physiological changes

Eg: Nitrates and ACEI induced postural hypotension in an elderly patient, grey baby syndrome with chloramphenicol in childrens

Drug characteristics: Some drugs are toxic in nature and patients treated with those agents are at increased risk of ADRs.

Eg: Nausea and vomiting with cytotoxic anticancer drugs

Patients treated with narrow therapeutic index drugs are more at risks

Gender: Women are reported to be more susceptible to ADRs than men

Eg: Chloramphenicol induced aplastic anaemia and phenylbutazone induced agranulocytosis are twice and thrice as common in women as in men respectively.

Race and genetic factors: More prone to ADRs in genetically predisposed individuals

Eg: Patients G6PD deficiency are at higher risk of developing haemolysis due to primaquine.

MECHANISM OF ADRS

Mechanism of type A **ADR** Any Type A reaction which occurs in an individual may be due to one of the following reasons:

Pharmaceutical causes

Pharmacokinetic causes

Pharmacodynamic causes

Mechanism of type A ADR

Pharmaceutical causes: Changes in the drug quantity present in a particular product

Changes in drug releasing properties

Eg: Griseofulvin having different particle size in final dosage form. Switching its larger particle size product with smaller one leads to toxicity by increasing peak concentration

Pharmacokinetic causes: Alteration in the ADME of drugs – changing concentration of drug at site of action

Absorption: changes in rate and extent of drug absorption

Distribution: changes in blood flow and protein or tissue binding

Metabolism: Reduced metabolism lead to higher rate of type A ADRs whereas therapeutic failure occurs as metabolism increases

Excretion: changes in drug excretion rate

Pharmacodynamic causes: Increased sensitivity of target tissues or organs

Drug receptors: inter-individual variation in drug receptor

Homeostatic mechanism: changes in physiological factors determine the extent of a drug's effect

Disease: Eg: asthmatic patient developing bronchoconstriction after taking non-selective beta blockers (Propranolol)

Mechanism of Type B ADR Any Type B reaction which occurs in an individual may be due to one of the following reasons: Pharmaceutical causes Pharmacokinetic causes Pharmacodynamic causes

Pharmaceutical causes: Decomposition of the active ingredients

Effects of drug excipients (Eg: propylene glycol and carboxymethylcellulose causes hypersensitivity)

Synthetic by product of active constituents

Death have been reported due to decomposition of paraldehyde to acetaldehyde and its subsequent oxidation to acetic acid.

Pharmacokinetic causes: Although pharmacokinetic changes lead to type B ADRs but there are no documented type B ADRs due to absorption and distribution.

Metabolism: unusual reactive drug metabolite leads to type B ADRs. Eg: Carbamazepine induced hypersensitivity reactions

Pharmacodynamic causes: Age, sex, body weight, medical condition and drug therapy influence the end response of a patient to an administered drug.

Genetic causes for abnormal responses: Eg G6PD deficiency results in hemolysis Immunological reasons for abnormal response

Teratological and neoplastic reasons for abnormal response.

Excessive pharmacological effects: these occurs due to the excess pharmacological activity of a drug caused by long-time use or drug overdose.

It is common in neonates, infants and elderly patients.

Some drugs cause excessive pharmacological effects even at normal doses in patients with kidney failure (who have lost 70% of kidney patients), Liver diseases, anaemia and patients with lower albumin level.

Ex: 1) Hypotensive agents in hypertension, excess dose causes profound hypotension.

2) Antihyperglycemic drugs in excess doses causes hypoglycemia.

3) Heparin/warfarin are the anticoagulant drugs but at higher doses may cause bleeding.

4) Barbiturates are the CNS depressant drugs but in excess doses it can cause coma

Secondary pharmacological effects: drugs have several pharmacological actions at usual therapeutic dose but it is prescribed solely or primarily for one of these beneficial actions.

It simply means the effect produced by the drug is different than the drug administered for particular purpose.

Ex: Anti-histamine drugs prescribed for their anti-allergic skin reactions or anti-nausea effects, but they produce drowsiness due to CNS depression. (which is its its secondary pharmacological effect)

This action may be important in case of patients lying on bed but, can causes difficulty if the patient is motor driver. • This condition may worsen if the patient is also taking hypnotic, tranquilizer, cough suppressants as medicines or if the patient is consuming alcohol. 2.

Rebound or return effect on stopping of drug: Use of long term of many medication produce tolerance or dependence at cellular level.

Sudden withdrawal of such medications may give rise to severe adverse effects. • This type of reactions are common with drugs which acting on CNS.

Ex. 1. CNS depressant drugs such as ethyl alcohol, barbiturates & benzodiazepines on withdrawal produce marked agitation, tachycardia, confusion, delirium and convulsions.

2. Some anti-hypertensive drugs such as clonidine used in hypertension but its sudden withdrawal may cause severe hypertension.

3. Withdrawal of anti-epileptic drugs may increase seizures. Tolerance and dependence forming drugs should be replaced with appropriate alternative drugs to prevent ADR.

Unpredictable or Dose Independent or Bizarre effects: This type of ADRs are rare and unpredictable.

These are those adverse drug reactions in which we can-not predict that it can be happens.

It only occurs in some patients due to their peculiarity (a strange/Unique characteristic, quality or habit)

It has nothing to do with drug's pharmacological action.

More dangerous and require immediate stopping of the drugs concerned. • Low incidence but have High mortality.

E.g. penicillin-G induced anaphylactic shock, hemolysis with primaquine. B.

Idiosyncrasy: The word Idiosyncrasy means a person's particular way of behaving, thinking, etc., especially an unusual characteristic.

Idiosyncrasy refers to inherent peculiarity of individual.

Drug induced diseases are included in these types of reactions.

Examples: 1. Thalidomide causes drug induces fetal abnormalities (phocomelia) in pregnant women's.

2. Drug induced cancer is an idiosyncrasy reaction like: i) long term use of estrogens produces uterine cancer ii) Administration of analgesic drugs to patients with renal disease may induce tumors of kidney pelvis).

Barbiturates produce excitement and mental confusion in some individuals instead of producing depression. 1.

Allergic drug reaction including Anaphylaxis: This is also called as drug hypersensitivity reactions.

It is important to note that not all patients experience allergic reactions to the drug. Only small percentage of the population goes through these reactions.

It includes all the reactions mediated by antigen-antibody reactions.

Drug acting as a foreign antigen which react with antibody in human body to cause undesirable effects like skin rashes, bronchospasm, anaphylactic shock, etc.

Different types of allergic reactions are produced in different individuals for the same drug and sometimes a completely different drug may produce the same type of reactions.

As already pointed out, they are unpredictable and not related to dose because sometimes an increase in dose cannot produce the same reaction in other individuals.

Examples: 1. Anaphylaxis (severe life-threatening allergic reaction that happens very sudden) reaction due to penicillin, anesthetic drugs and due to iodine containing compounds. 2. Haemolytic anaemia (RBC destruction) due to penicillin and sulphonamides.

3. Leucopenia (WBC destruction) due to sulphonamides and phenylbutazone.

4. Thrombocytopenia (low level of platelets in blood) due to quinidine, digoxin and thiazide

3. Genetically determined toxicity: Patients genetic make-up are at greater risk for specific drug toxicities. Genotype of a particular individual can cause variation in the effects of drugs, hence there are possibilities of ADR. Due to individual variations the drug pharmacokinetic and pharmacodynamic actions are slightly different. Sometimes, to produce the same effect, an increase of 500% in dose may be required for some individuals depending on their genetics. It is because their rate of metabolism differs and we know that the rate of metabolism depends on microsomal enzyme which in turn, is controlled by genes. The site of action and its sensitivity to drugs also play an important role in the drug's effect which differs due to genotypes.

Example: 1. Many drugs are detoxified in liver by acetylation: The ability of acetylation of many drugs in liver is variable in individuals. Slow acetylators have greater risk of toxicity for some drugs like- isoniazide, procainamide, hydralazine, phenelzine and dapsone.

2. Glucose-6-phosphate dehydrogenase is involved in pentose phosphate pathway: Some populations in Africa and south east Asia are deficient in this enzyme and therefore there is risk of developing hemolytic anemia (breakdown of RBCs) after the use of antimalarial drugs like primaquine, sulphonamides, guanidine & nitrofurantoin. (Pentose phosphate pathway helps protect RBCs from oxidative damage)

Drug Interactions: Drug interactions are the part of adverse drug reactions. Drug interactions are defined as the pharmacological action of the one drug is altered by the simultaneous use of another drug or the presence of some other substances like food, alcohol, smoking or presence of existing morbidity. This reaction can be synergistic (when the drug effect is increased) or antagonistic (when the drug effect is decreased) or new effect can be produced that neither produces on its own.

Classification of drug interactions: depending on the benefit and some other factors, drug interactions are classified into two types. 1. Beneficial interactions 2. Adverse interactions

1. Beneficial interactions: These interactions are also known as rational interactions. • Few drugs, on interaction with other drugs produce beneficial effects. • Some drugs are used purposely to enhance the effect of other drugs or to minimize the unwanted effect of it. • There are many formulations in the market using these beneficial effects are: 1. Sulphamethoxazole and trimethoprim combination (Co-Trimoxazole) used as an anti-microbial to treat and prevent many bacterial infections like UTIs, bronchitis, prostatitis. 2. Carbidopa and levodopa combination is used to treat Parkinson's disease. 3. Estrogen-progestogen combination pill is used as contraceptive. 4. Ampicillin and cloxacillin combination is used as potent antibiotic. 1.

Drug interactions can also be used to treat patients struggling with the drug overdose as they nullify or antagonize the adverse effects of overdose drug.

1. Levodopa & Vitamin B6: levodopa is a dopamine precursor used in management of Parkinson's disease whose overdose causes severe dizziness, irregular heartbeat, mental/mood changes etc. (vitamin B6 supplements reduces the effectiveness of levodopa).

2. Warfarin and Vitamin K: warfarin is an anti-coagulant drug which is used to prevent clotting whose overdose can cause life threatening bleeding. In such cases vitamin-k is used as an antidote which brings homeostasis.

2. Adverse interactions: This interaction is also known as irrational interactions. • These interactions are undesired and harmful to the patients • The adverse interactions are classified into three classes: 1. Pharmacokinetic drug interactions 2. Pharmacodynamic drug interactions 3. Miscellaneous drug interactions

i. Pharmacokinetic drug interactions:

These are the interactions which occurs due to ADME of a drug

a. Interactions affecting absorption of drug: • One drug may decrease the absorption of another drug through GIT. E.g. absorption of tetracycline may get decrease if the antacid is run simultaneously, because tetracycline forms inactive complex with calcium and magnesium ions presents in antacid.

b. Interactions affecting distribution of drug: • These interactions mainly include the change in protein binding of drug. E.g. Phenyl-butanone replaces the tolbutamide from the protein binding and increases the hypoglycemic effect of tolbutamide.

c. Interactions affecting metabolism/biotransformation of drug: one drug may alter the metabolism of other drug either by enzyme induction or by enzyme inhibition. Enzyme induction: barbiturate stimulates the enzyme system present within the liver and thus, increases the metabolism of the other drugs like alcohol, anticoagulant. Enzyme inhibition: Disulfiram inhibits the metabolism of alcohol.

d. Interaction affecting excretion/elimination of drug: one drug may affect excretion of another drug. Increase in excretion: antacids like bicarbonate of soda makes the urine alkaline and increases the ionization of acidic drug salicylates and thus, results in rapid excretion. Decrease in excretion: probenecid competes with penicillin for excretion, and thus inhibits excretion of penicillin.

ii. Pharmacodynamic drug interactions: These interactions happen when two drugs with same or opposing pharmacological effects are concurrently administered unknowingly. a. antagonism: the interacting drugs have opposing actions. e.g. acetylcholine and nor-adrenaline have opposing effects on heart rate b. addition/summation: the interacting drugs have similar actions and the resultant effects is the sum of individual drug responses. e.g. CNS depressants like sedative and hypnotics. c. synergism/potentiation: it is an enhancement of action of one drug by another. e.g. alcohol enhances the analgesics activity of aspirin.

iii. Miscellaneous drug interactions:

Drug-drug interactions: These interactions occur when two or more drugs interact with one another. Interaction can occur with prescribed drugs, OTC drugs, vitamins and alternative medications like supplements and herbal products. Examples: 1. Warfarin + Aspirin: excessive bleeding-(synergism effect) 2. Warfarin + phenobarbital: less anticoagulant effect-(antagonism effect) 3. Codeine + Paracetamol: increased analgesic effect- (addition effect)

b. Drug-food interactions: In these interactions the effect of drug may change because of the presence of certain foods items in GIT. Examples: 1. Aspirin + milk: upset stomach, 2. Tetracycline + calcium food: reduced absorption of drug 3. MAO inhibitors therapy shouldn't eat the food items like banana, cheese, chocolate, etc. as these items contains great quantity of tyramine. (serious spike in blood pressure which requires emergency treatment)

Drug-disease interaction: This type of interaction occurs when a drug worsens or exacerbates an existing medical condition (disease) Examples: 1. Hypertension + nasal decongestants: increased hypertension 2. Asthma patients + NSAIDs: airway obstruction 3. Hypertension + nicotine: increased heart rate

Reporting of ADRs: Healthcare professionals should report ADR only when they found that the administered drug has suspicious connections which cause a particular adverse event.

What to report?

Who should report?

When to report?

How to report?

Whom to report?

1. **What to report?** All adverse events should be reported

    Report non-serious, known or unknown, frequent or rare adverse drug reactions due to Medicines, Vaccines & Herbal Products.

Report every serious adverse drug reactions. A reaction is serious when the patient outcome is:

Death

Life-threatening

Hospitalization (initial or prolonged)

Disability (significant, persistent or permanent)

Congenital anomaly

Report intervention to prevent permanent impairment or damage

Include all ADRs as a result of prescription or non-prescription drugs.

All suspected ADRs associated with drug-drug and drug-food interactions.

ADRs occurring from overdose of drug or error of medication.

ADRs in special field of interests such as drug use in pregnancy and lactation.

ADRs in drug abuse.

2. Who should report? All the Health care practioners such as doctors, dentists, pharmacists, nurses, assistant medical officers, clinical officers, pharmaceutical technicians, pharmaceutical assistants & traditional medical practitioners.

2. All government hospitals, health centres, private hospitals, pharmacies, dispensaries, private clinics, and nursing homes have compulsion to report all ADR cases which are reported to them by the patients.

3. When to report? Any suspected ADR should be reported as soon as possible by the healthcare professionals. 2. Delay in reporting will made reporting inaccurate and unreliable. 3. If the patient is still in hospital, then it is right time to report the suspected ADRs because reporter can clear any doubts from patients by re-questioning and re-examining the patient.

4. How to report? Reporter should report ADRs Via suspected ADR reporting form of AMC (Adverse drug reaction Monitoring Center) or NCC (National Coordinating Center). This form include: 1. Patient information (patient identity, birth date/age, gender and weight in kg) 2. Suspected ADR: date of reaction started, date of recovery, describe the reaction or problem, relevant tests/laboratory data with dates, other relevant history including pre-existing medical conditions (e.g. Allergies, race, pregnancy, smoking, alcohol use, hepatic/renal dysfunctions, etc.), seriousness of the reaction and outcomes) 3. Suspected medications related information 4. Reporter information (name, address, e-mail, phone no., occupation, signature, date of report, etc.)

_5. Where to report? <u>Filled the </u>Suspected Adverse drug reaction form can be sent to the nearest Adverse drug reaction Monitoring Centre (AMC) or directly to the National Coordination Centre (NCC).

2. Call on Helpline (Toll Free) no. 1800 180 3024 to report ADRs.

3. Directly mail this filled form to pvpi@ipcindia.net or pvpi.ipcindia@gmail.com

4. A list of nationwide AMCs is available at: http://www.ipc.gov.in or http://www.ipc.gov.in/PvPI/pv-home.html.

COMMUNITY PHARMACY

<u>As the</u> name indicates, a community pharmacy is an organization functioning in the aid of a community of an area and provides drug and other health services to the people.

Definition: Community pharmacy is defined as an organization that is privately owned and whose functions in varying degrees, is to serve society's need for both drug products and pharmaceutical services" Functions include: procurement, storage, compounding, dispensing of prescription & OTC drugs with care, accuracy, & legality and also provide pharmaceutical services like counselling, provide education, training, etc.

The community pharmacies in India are still traditional, mostly product-oriented and functioning with a commercial background. On the other hand, developed countries have modern community pharmacies that are patient- oriented and providing pharmaceutical care to the people. This is because those pharmacies have highly qualified (M. pharm or Pharm.D) pharmacists, unlike D. pharm pharmacists we have in India.

Organization and structure of retail and wholesale drug store

Manufacturer/Producer → Wholesaler → Retailer → Consumer One of the main factors responsible for the success of a drug store is its location and proper layout design.

Location: <u>Best site</u> for a pharmacy is the place where most patients visit nearby practicing physicians. So, it should be established in a place close to the clinics of practicing physicians. The next best site could be near the heart of the village, town or a city where a lot of people go shopping and the floating population is more. Here, the people bring the prescription for purchase, old prescriptions of refilling, or for OTC medicines. • The third viable site to establish a pharmacy is in a newly developed area or the colonies of cities where a considerable no. of people live. As the area of residence grows and spreads, the community pharmacy gets the advantage. Here, the growth is slow but steady.

Layout Design: A modern drug store should fulfill all the requirements in schedule 'N' of the Drug & cosmetic rules 1945. To start a retail drug store a minimum of 150 sq. meter area is required. Similarly to wholesale drug store a minimum of 200 sq. meter area is required.

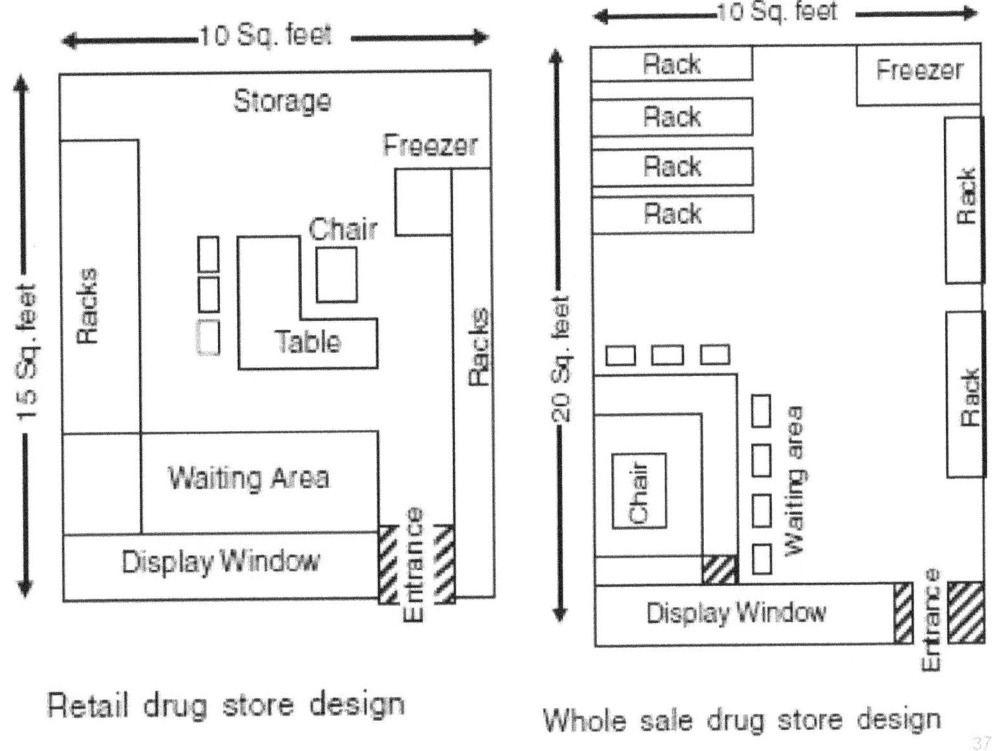

Generally, the drug stores are located on ground floor of the building. • The outer front of the drug store should be very attractive and built with innovated construction technique. • The material used for construction drug store front is normally glass, glazed tiles and marbles which is easy to clean. • They are usually constructed of cement concrete walls & mosaic tiles on the floor. • The floor of the drug store should be smooth and washable. • The internal fitting usually consists of racks or proper storage cupboards with glass doors, drawers for storing strips, shelves and proper place for placing refrigerator. • The furniture includes a counter, working table, wooden or steel chairs for staff and customers.

Retail Drug Store: Good lightning system provides cheerful atmosphere for customers it also helps in identifying the medicines quickly and easily and thus increase the efficiency of the store. The illumination should be steady and should not put any strain on the eyes.

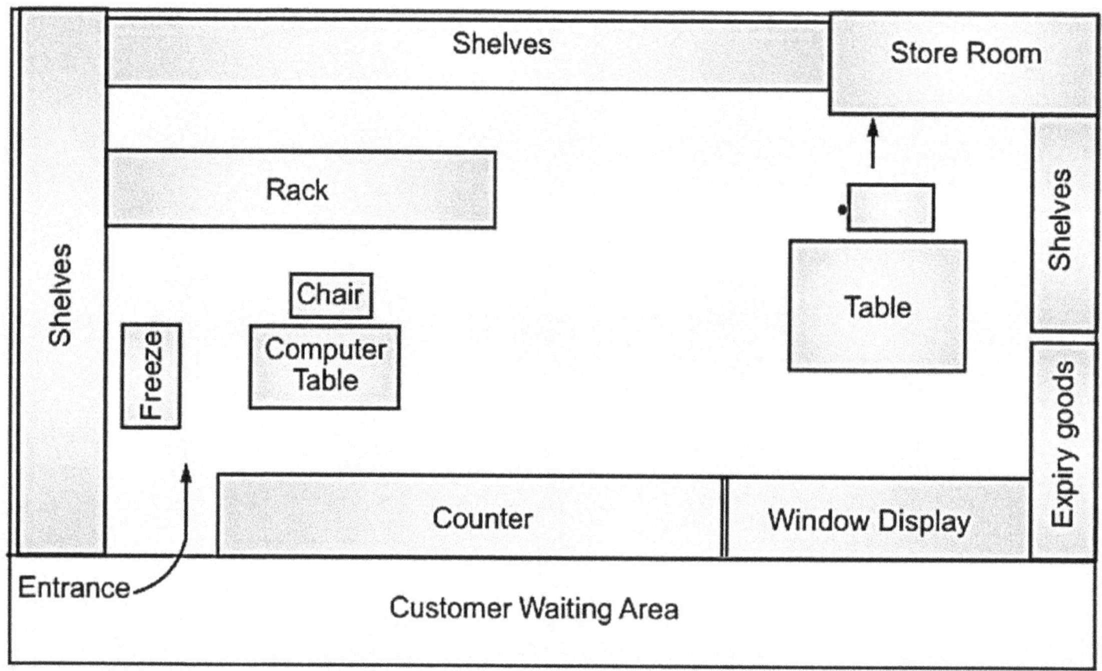

Layout of Retail Pharmacy Store

Objectives of Layout Design:

To attract a large number of customers

To increase the sale of store

To reduce the selling expenses to a minimum

To provide the customer satisfaction

To have adequate space for reserve stock, office and resting place for the employees

To have proper entrance for coming goods

To project a professional image and improve general appearance

To minimize the movement of customers within the premises of the drug store

Types of Drug Stores

Based on the layout & design community drug stores are classified as: Drug Store Types

1. Traditional drug stores

2. Personal service drug stores

3. Prescription oriented drug store

4. Pharmaceutical Centre

5. Super drug store

1. Traditional drug stores: These types of drug stores are designed in such a way that the whole area of the drug store is exposed to customers. • Such a design has a pleasing & professional appearance and is convenient for both workers & customers

2. Personal service drug stores: In these types of stores the whole area is not exposed to the customer but the customer is required to interact with the drug store personnel at the service counter. During the purchasing process the customer demands an article and thc Personnel provide the articles. This design offers maximum facilities and interaction between drug store employee and customers. The success of these type of drug store depends upon the convenience & Friendly service of the personnel at the service counter.

Prescription oriented drug store: They provide a comfortable waiting area where the customers are expected to wait while his prescription is proceeding. • In this design health related items, drugs and prescription accessories are displayed in the vicinity while orthopedics and surgical appliances are kept in a separate room. • Cosmetics and gifts are arranged in a suitable area in the store of this type.

4. Pharmaceutical centre: These types of stores sell medicines, convenience articles orthopedic and surgical appliances

5. Super drug store: Drug stores have a huge floor area ranging from 5,000 to 10,000 with a square design. Their customers have access to almost all the area in the drug store and can inspect, handle and select articles themselves. The design is on self-service pattern except for the prescription department where self-service is not possible.

Legal requirements for establishment and maintenance of drug store

1. Minimum qualification:

A person who wishes to start a retail drug store should be a registered pharmacist in state pharmacy council or PCI. Along with registered pharmacist he should fulfill the requirements given in Pharmacy Act such as:

    i.   The person should attain at least 18 years of age

    ii.   ii. He should be a resident of the state or should be carrying out his business/profession of pharmacy in state

    iii.   iii. Should possess a degree or diploma in pharmacy or any other approved qualification, from a institute recognized by PCI. A person who wishes to start a wholesale drug store may not be a registered pharmacists but must have passed at least matriculation examination and must possess at least 4 years of experience in handling of drugs.

2. Minimum space: As per schedule N of Drug and cosmetic act 1940 the minimum area required to start a retail drug store are 150 sq. meter and wholesale drug store are 200 sq. meter **3. Store arrangement:** The area should be equipped with proper storage facility for preserving the properties of drug.

For storage of thermolabile substances such as vaccines, sera, enzymatic preparations, antibiotics vitamins, etc. a refrigerator is required in order to store these drugs at temp. between 2°C to 8°C. There should be sufficient no. of storage racks for storing of drugs and pharmaceuticals. • The requirements as specified in schedule M, to the Drug & cosmetic act should be fulfilled.

4. Application & Forms required: • An Application to the drug inspector in the form of request + Form no.19 (application for grant or renewal of license to sell, stock, exhibit or distribute drugs) **a. License for retail: b. License for wholesale:** Form 20 For drugs other than those specified in schedule C & C1 Form 21 For drugs specified in schedule C & C1 Form 20 F For drugs specified in schedule X Form 20 B For drugs other than those specified in schedule C & C1 Form 21 B For drugs specified in schedule C & C1 Form 20 G For drugs specified in schedule X

5. Other documents required: 1. Self-attested copy of Registration certificate of pharmacist issued by state pharmacy council/PCI 2. Self-attested copy of proof of passing the diploma/degree course in pharmacy from institute recognized by PCI 3. An attested copy of matriculation certificate as a proof of date of birth. 4. Proof of ownership if the applicant is the owner of premices, or if the premices are on rent, then a copy of the rent receipt is attached with the application form. 5. NOC from local area authority. 6. Map/layout of store

7. In case of two or more persons are partners for starting drug store then a copy of partnership is to be attached with application.

8. Experience certificate of applicant not less than 4 years in case of wholesale drug store.

Dispensing of Proprietary Medicines:

1. What is Dispensing? Dispensing is a main part of pharmacy practice in which the distributor/pharmacist takes the required order of medicine from physician on the prescription and accordingly supplies the medicines for the treatment of patients.

2. What are proprietary medicines? Proprietary medicines are the such chemical substances which are used for medicinal purposes and are formulated or manufactured under a name protected from competition through copyright, trademark or patent.

3. Flow of dispensing procedure are as follows:

1. Receiving the order of proprietary drug (e.g. Amlodipine). Check whether this order received correctly.

2. Keep the received order at side and check for expiry date and storage conditions

3. Find the location of the shelf for the received order. Location should not be confused with other available stock.

4. Receive the order (Amlodipine) of prescription and locate the medicine for dispensing. During locating of medicine, dispenser should check the medicine for correctness because there may similarly sounding medicine present next to it (e.g. Amitriptyline)

5. Identify and pick the correct medicine. Check the medicine strength and quantity as per the order received from physician

6. Before dispensing the medicine, check the label and instructions given on the label and same to be instruct to patients. (by orally or in written format)

7. Hand out the medicine to patient. Check the right patient to whom the right medicine is hand out.

Maintenance of records of retail and wholesale drug store

To open any drug store (retail or wholesale) the owner of drug store should have to maintain various records and documentation. • There are three types of records maintained by drug traders out of which the first two are common for both retail and wholesale trades and the third one is for the retail pharmacy only.

A. Legal records

B. Financial records

C. Patient records

A. Legal records:

All the legal requirements related information such as refrigerators, HVAC systems, proper storage conditions are maintained in legal records. According to federal and state law the pharmacy owner or manager is charged with maintaining accurate up-to-date records of specific classes of drugs and poisons. Under the provisions of the Federal Controlled Substances Act of 1970, the pharmacists are charged for maintaining accurate records related to the acquisition and disposition of certain drugs.

Legal records include: Purchase records, stock register, Sales register, Prescription file for schedule x drugs, Inspection register, Communication file.

1. Purchase records: Records regarding purchase of all drugs whether intended to be sold in retail or by wholesale should be maintained: 1. Date of purchase 2. Name & address of the licensee from whom purchased and his license no. 3. Name & quantity of the drug 4. Name of the manufacturer of drug and its batch no. • Purchase bills including cash or credit memos should be kept as records.

2. Stock register: Maintain records of all drugs present in storage section.

3. Sales register

Maintain records of sale of drugs specified in schedule x and sale of drugs other than those

Sale of drugs specified in schedule x

Date of purchase

The name and address of supplier and the license no. of the supplier

Name & quantity of the drug supplied

Manufacturers name, batch or lot number

Name & address of the patient/purchaser

Reference no. of the prescription against which supplies were made

Bill no. & date of receipt of purchase or supply made by him

Sale of drugs other than those specified in schedule x

Serial no. of the entry

Date of supply

Name & address of the purchaser

Name & address of the patient or the name & address of the owner of the animal, if the drug is supplied for veterinary use

Name along with the quantities of drug supplied

In case of schedule H and C drugs, the name of the manufacturer, its batch no. and the expiry date, if any.

Signature of the registered pharmacist under whose supervision the medicine was made or supplied.

3. Sales register:

4. Prescription file for schedule x drugs: Such prescriptions in which physicians prescribe schedule x drugs to patients are maintained in record only in case of retail stores.

5. Inspection register: All the legal data are maintained in this register regarding the drug store, its license and personnel working, etc.

6. Communication file: Official letters and circulars from drug control and other government departments.

B. Financial records: Maintains information regarding the past and present financial status of pharmacy These records are required to run the pharmacy efficiently. Essential for making decisions regarding future money needs, personnel matters, expansion of facilities, etc.

Financial records include: 1. Daybook 2. Journal 3. Ledger 4. Profit and loss account including trial balance and balance sheet. 5. Tax notices, receipts and other particulars file (income tax, GST, etc.) 6. Insurance file 7. Salary registers 8. Miscellaneous file (rent, electric bill, telephone bill, etc.) 9. Employees service and leave register. 10. Also include purchase, sale and stock registers which are already discussed in legal records.

C. Patient records: These are maintained by few pharmacies only.

Specially the modern pharmacies which offers patient-oriented services to earn name, fame and goodwill and thereby they make money from these value-added services.

Some pharmacies also record patient data to reduce the drug interactions and problems associated with individual drugs.

Patient records include: 1. Patient medication profile (history) 2. Patients' family members medication profile 3. Copies of important prescriptions, lab reports, etc. of selected patients for future reference, guidance and counselling.

All the above records are maintained as hard copies wherever necessary & also as soft copies in pharmacy computers with facilities for easy retrieval.

DRUG DISTRIBUTION SYSTEM IN A HOSPITAL

Hospital pharmacy may be defined as that department of the hospital which deals with procurement, storage, compounding, dispensing, manufacturing, testing, packing, and distribution of drugs.

Functions

Proper storing of drugs.

Providing specifications for the purchase of drugs, chemicals.

Manufacturing &distribution of medicaments such as parenteral products, tablets, capsules, ointments & stock mix.

In-patient:

In-patients are those patients, who require hospitalization i.e get themselves admitted in the hospital, stay there for treatment till they are discharged. They are four systems in general use for dispensing drugs for inpatients.

They may be classified as follows;

1. Individual prescription order

2.Complete floor stock system

3. Combination of individual &floor stock system

4. Unit dose system

1. Individual prescription order system: It is a type of prescription system where the physician writes the prescription for individual patient who obtains the drug prescribed from any medical store or hospital dispensary by paying own charges.

Advantages: All medication orders are directly reviewed by pharmacists. It provides the interaction of pharmacist-doctor, nurse and the patient. It provides clear control of inventory.

2. Complete floor stock system: Under this system, the drugs are given to the patient through the nursing station and the pharmacy supplies from the drug store of a hospital. in to.

Drugs on the nursing station or ward may be divided

A. Charge floor stock drugs

B. Non charge floor stock drugs.

a. Charge floor stock system: Medicines which are stocked on the nursing station at all times and charged to the patient's account after they have been administered to them.

Dispensing of floor stock drugs.

The patient is charged for every single dose administered to him.

Selection of these drugs in various wards is decided by PTC

Once the floor stock list is prepared ,it becomes the responsibility of the hospital pharmacist to make the drugs available.

Pharmaceutical and related preparation

Category	Preparation
Anti allergies	Prednisolone tablet
Antibiotics	Penicillin G
Anticoagulant	inj. heparin
Cardio vascular agents	Digoxin inj.

A label for a charge floor stock: Ward- Phenobarbitone tablets. Each tablet contains Each tablet contains Phenobarbitone -50g Phenobarbitone -50g

b.Non-charge floor stock drugs: Non charge floor stock drugs are the medicaments that are placed at the nursing station for the use of all patients on the floor.

These drugs, there shall be no direct charge from the patient's account. It is divided in to two methods.

 a. Drug basket method.

b. Mobile dispensary unit.

Drug basket method:

Nurse fills a requisition form for delivery of drugs at their floor;

When there is an empty container, the nurse place it in the drug basket.

Once the basket is completed, it delivery to the floor via messenger service.

Alternatively mobile dispensary can be utilised.

Mobile dispensary:

It is specially constructed stainless steel.

60 inches high.

48 inches wide and 25 inches deep.

It is mounted on bottom tyres.

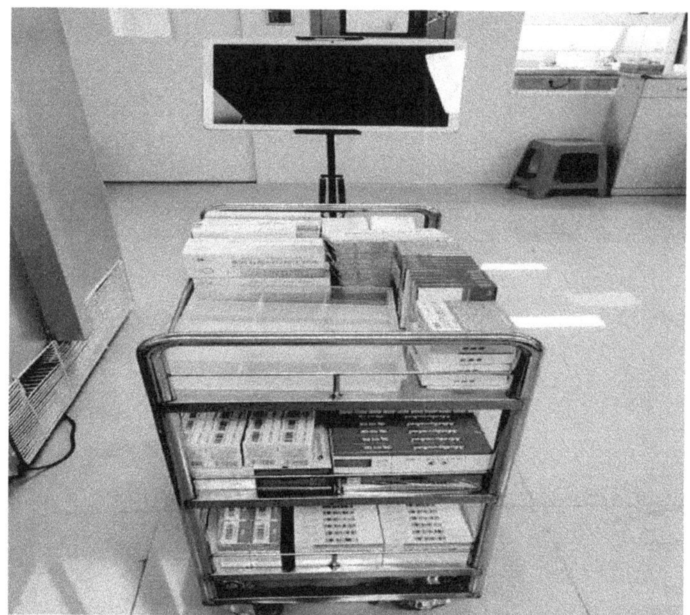

Label for non-charge floor stock drug: Ward- Ward- Ferrous sulphate tablets Ferrous sulphate tablets Each tablet contains: Ferrous sulphate 0.3gm.

Following list of such non-charge drugs

Ampoules	Capsules	Tablets	Solutions	Powders
adrenaline	dulcolax	Atropine sulphate	Tin.belladona	glucose
digoxin	multivitamins	Paracetamol	Castor oil	Sodium bicarbonate
Lidocaine HCl	digitalis	nitroglycerine	Tin.benzoin compound	talcum
aminophylline			Elixir kcl	

Difference between floor & non floor stock system Charge floor stock system

Charge floor stock system	Non-charge floor stock system
The charges are made in the patients account after the have been administered from the stock drugs.	The drugs are not made in the account directly even after the drug have been administered.
Every dose of the drug administered to the patients are charged.	This system charges are made indirectly to the patients.
Only those doses are charged which are expansive can rarely use.	The cost of the drugs is not high as they are mostly used in tablets, capsules.
Floor stock list is prepared which is sent to make the drugs available to all the nursing station	A pre-determined list is prepared by nursing station.

3. Combination of individual and floor stock system:

This system is fallowed in the government and also in private hospital who run on the basis of no profit and no loss.

Individual prescription or medication system is fallowed as a major means.

Requirement of drugs or surgical items are given to the patient who purchase and deposit these items in hospital wards or rooms under supervision of registered nurse.

4. Unit dose dispensing:

Those medications which are ordered, packed, handled administered and charged in multiples of single dose units containing a predetermined amount of drug or supply sufficient for one regular dose.

A single unit package is one which contains one complete pharmaceutical dosage forms Ex-one tablet, capsule.

Advantages: Better financial control. It prevents the loss of partially used medications. It does not require storage facilities at the nursing station.

Two methods of dispensing unit doses are:

    A. Centralised unit-dose drug distribution system (CUDD)

    B. Decentralized unit-dose drug distribution system (DUDD)

A. Centralised unit-dose drug distribution system (CUDD): All in-patient drugs are dispensed in unit doses and all the drugs are stored in central area of the to be given to the patient. pharmacy and dispensed at the time the dose is due to be given to the patient

Drugs re transferred from the pharmacy to the indoor patient by medication cards.

B. Decentralized unit dose dispensing: This operates through small satellite pharmacies located on each floor of the hospital. Procedure: Patient profile card containing full date, disease, diagnosis is prepared. Prescription is sent directly to the pharmacist which are then entered in the patient profile card. Pharmacist checks medication order. Patient profile card and prescription order is filled by pharmacy technicians. The nurses administer the drugs and make the entry in their records.

Advantages: Easy for the administration staff, accounting becomes easier in certain cases, better stability of the products Ex-Eno-fruit salt in sachets.

Disadvantages: High cost, consumes more time and doubtful, will occupy more space for storing, ledger posting and inventory control problem.

General flow chart for In-patients

Out-patient: Outpatient refers to patients not occupying beds in a hospital or in clinics, health centres and other places out patient load into three categories

Emergency

Tertiary care

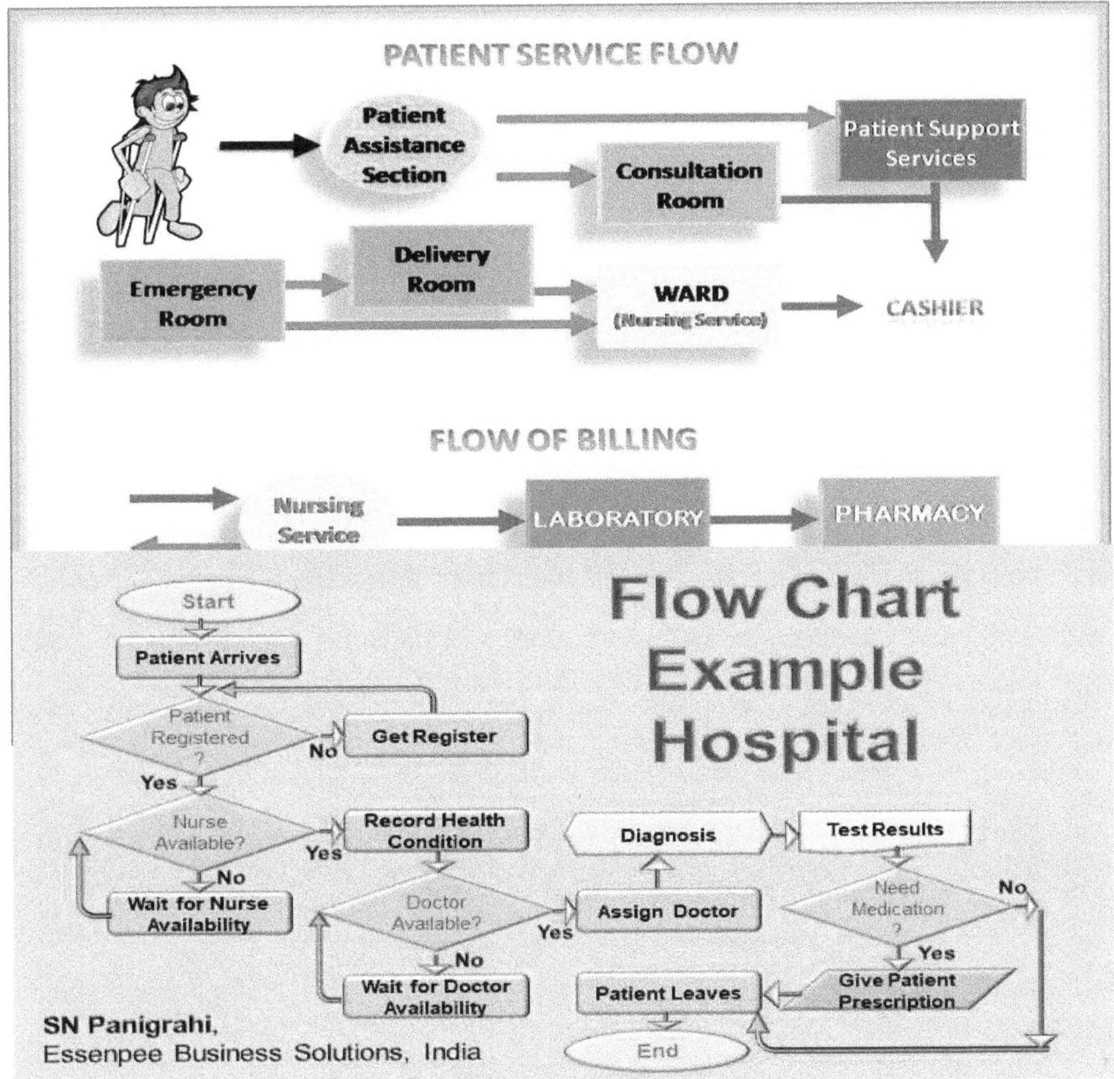

Emergency: A person given emergency or accidental care for conditions which require immediate medical attention. Suffering from serious health conditions or illness.

A person given emergency or accidental care for conditions which require immediate medical attention. Suffering from serious health conditions or illness.

Tertiary care: He is directly to outpatient department by his attending medical practitioner for specific treatment other than an emergency treatment.

Primary care: Primary care is majority care. It describes a range of services adequate for meeting.

Most primary care is used by patients who are ambulatory i.e are able to move about freely.

Location of out-patient dispensing: It should be located on the ground floor of the building. with proper seating arrangement. The outpatient dispensing area should be provided. The pharmacy receives its supplies from medical stores weekly but emergency supplies can be obtained at any time.

Layout of out-patient department (OPD)

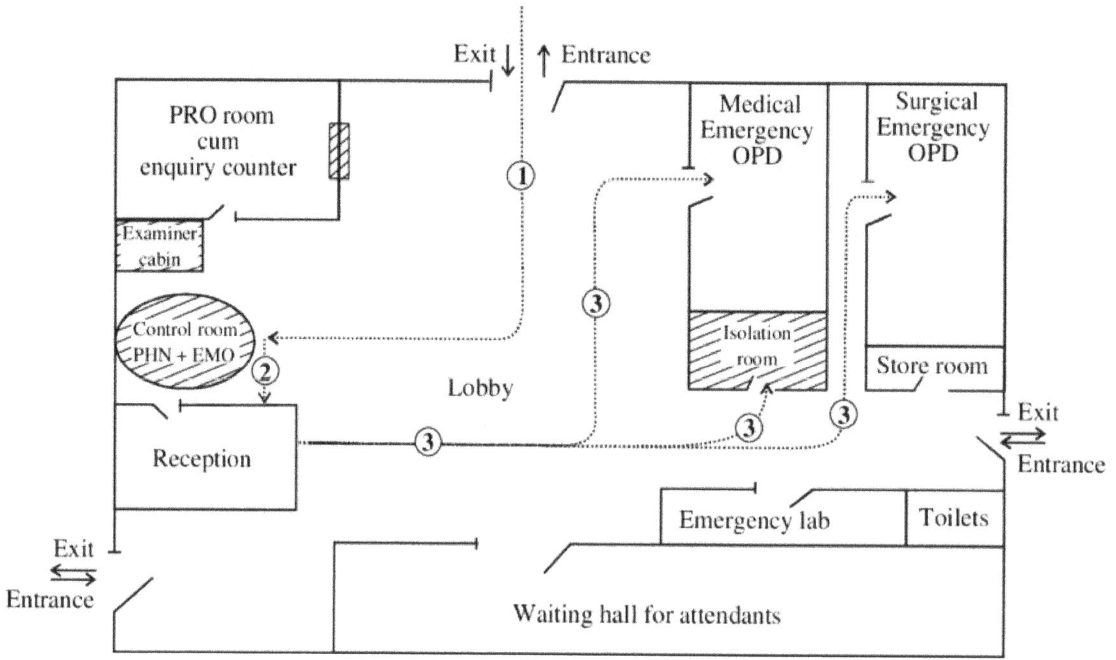

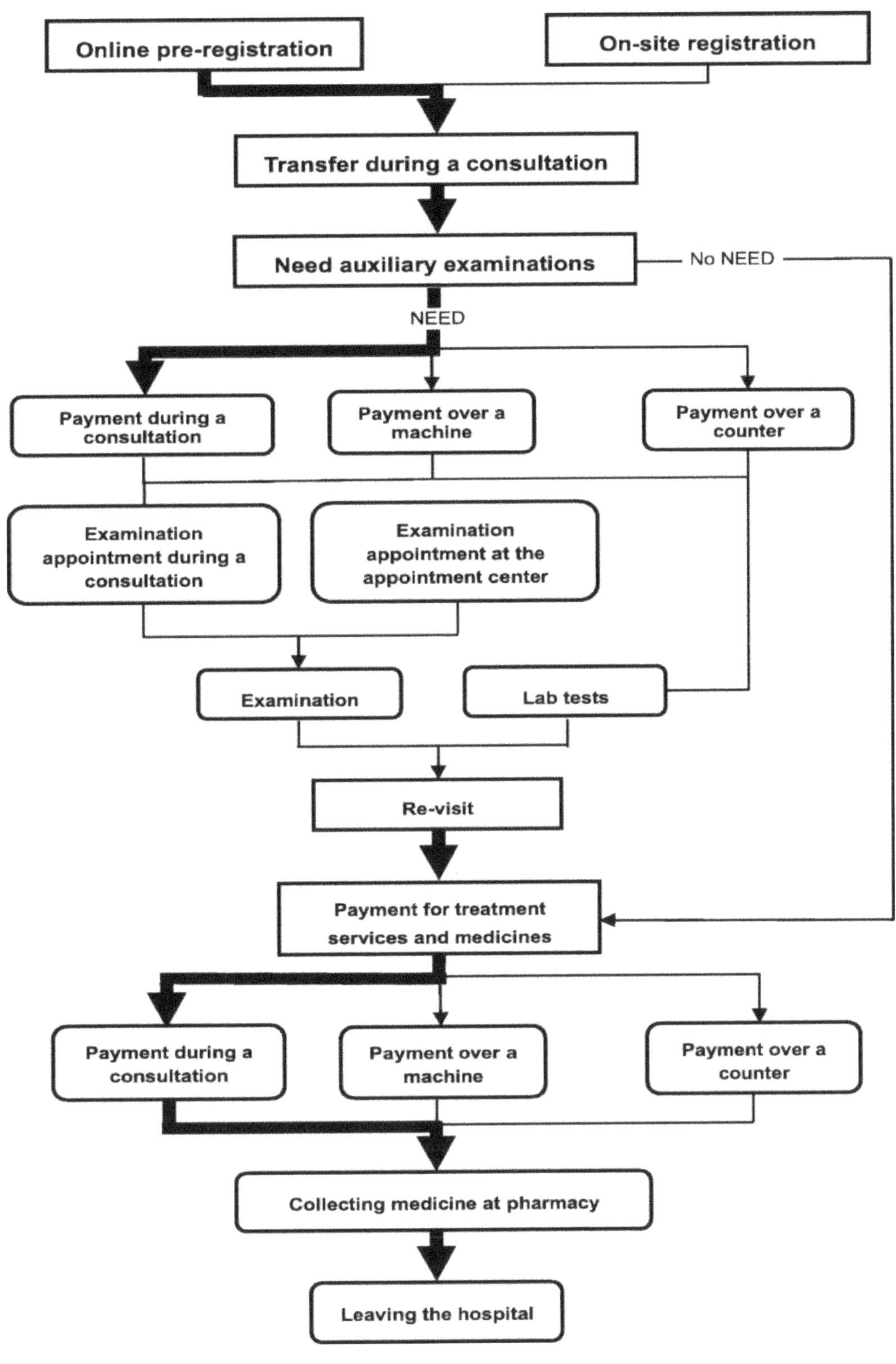

Out-patient activity chart

Drug distribution to out-patient: No medicaments should be issued without the prescription. After the issue has been made the quantities supplied must be recorded. Medicines are given to the out- patients from the pharmacy situated in the outpatient block.

Dispensing of control drugs:

Hospital control procedures:

1. Responsibility for controlled substance in the hospital. from the pharmacy.

2. Ordering ward stock of the controlled substances

3. Doctros orders for administration of controlled drugs.

Responsibility for controlled substances: The administrative head of the hospital is responsible for the proper safeguarding and the handling of controlled substances within the hospital.

Ordering ward stock of the controlled substances from the pharmacy:

a. A requisition forward stock-controlled substances desired. is completed by insertion a check mark opposite the name, strength from of controlled substance

b. Before any new controlled substances is issued to a ward

ABC Hospital, New Delhi						
Daily Controlled Drugs Administration Form Part-1						
Date ______ Ward No. __________ Floor __________						
Patient's Name	Specific Description of Drug	No. of Tablets or Injections	Strength Used	Ordered by Doctor	Adm. by Nurse	Time Given

Signature of Nurse __________

ABC Hospital, New Delhi					
Part-2					
Daily Controlled Drugs Administration Form Summary of Daily Report					
Name of the Tablets or Injections	Opening Day Record	Received	Total	Drugs Used	Balance

Signature of Nurse __________

Doctros orders for administration of controlled drugs: The fallowing information must appear on the "Doctor's controlled drug order sheet".

<u>ORDER FOR CONTROLLED DRUGS</u>

Serial No. 001

...............................NINEWELLS.. Hospital

Ward or Department ....18...............................

Name of Preparation	Strength	Quantity
MORPHINE SULFATE M /R TABLETS (MST)	60mg SIXTY MILLIGRAMS	60 (SIXTY) TABLETS

Ordered by ......*Linda Smith*......................LINDA SMITH............... Date ...24-APR-2020...........

    (Signature of Sister or Acting Sister)   (Print name above)

Supplied by .... Date ....

    (Pharmacists Signature)

Accepted for delivery .... Date ....

    (Signature of Messenger)

<u>TO BE RETAINED IN THE PHARMACEUTICAL DEPARTMENT</u>

Charging Policy All the hospitals should have a uniform charging policy for drugs. An unbiased price for drugs should be charged to all the patients while considering the financial interests of the hospital.

The charging policies are categorized under the following heads: **Per Diem Drug Charge or all Inclusive or no Special Rate:** In this system, charges for 250 patients are studied and their average daily charges for drugs and pharmaceutical services are calculated. On comparing the actual charge with the projected perdiem rate, the same revenue will be obtained as the itemized charging method. This system provides superior pharmaceutical services and also reduces the administrative and accounting cost of hospitals.

Part-Inclusive Rate: In this system, charges are made for drugs not on the free or supplied list.

Professional Fee Concept: This is the exclusive professional fee for all the operating expenses (including overhead and compensation) but not the actual cost of drug and container. This concept is being employed as it recovers expenses of pharmacy and total hospital expense. This fee concept should not be combined with mark-up or margin as these terms indicate that a percentage of wholesale or selling price is used as a base for the recovery of direct and indirect expenses.

Charging Policy

Break-Even Point Pricing: It is a useful tool in overall analysis of cost volume relationship and is defined on the level at which there is neither profit nor loss. For this, pharmacist should ascertain the fixed and indirect expenses including expenses of hospital administration, maintenance, housekeeping, depreciation of plant and equipment. Various costs, like housekeeping costs, and overhead costs (administration, light, water), are calculated by dividing the actual cost of these services by the number of prescriptions filled.

Cost-Plus Rate System: In this system, pharmacist maintains a better control using the formula: It helps in the adjustment of cost fluctuation, difference in currency value, and financial requirement. It offers fairness to the hospital and patients.

Profit Aspect: In this, profit is calculated into price to the patient by the following ways:

A fixed fee per prescription, and

Addition of predetermined percentage of the break-even point figure.

Computerized Pricing: This system is quite fair and provides computerized on -line pharmacy pricing.

The computer program will ask for the following information:

Patient number,

Drug identification number,

Dose factor, and Total number of doses dispensed.

Labelling

Legible: The information on the label should be either type- written or printed to make it easily readable.

Intelligible: The information on the label should be unmistakable to avoid any confusion.

Adequate and Relevant: The information on the label should be sufficiently relevant to avoid confusion. Limited but clear information should be provided on the label to make it noticeable. The label should comply with the requirements mentioned in the Drugs and Cosmetics Act and Rules and with current professional opinions.

Preparation of Labels for Dispensed Medicines

The following information should be provided by the label on the dispensed medicines:

Name and Address of the Patient: The first name(s) or initial(s) and surname of the patient should be put on the label of each dispensed medicine to avoid confusion with other members of the patient's family who might be taking similar medicines.

Name and Address of the Supplier and Date of Supply: The name and address of the pharmacy from where the drug is dispensed is pre-printed on the labels. The supply date is also mentioned on the label.

Precise Details Regarding the Contents of Container when Dispensed:

Name of the Medicine: The name and strength of the dispensed medicine is mentioned on the label for safety purpose; however, sometimes it causes unnecessary anxiety and distress to the patients. The preparation name written by the prescriber (whether proprietary name, non -proprietary name, official drugs given in I.P., B.P., U.S.P., B.P.C., B.N.F., etc.) should be on the label. ☐ If the prescriber uses a non-proprietary name for a preparation, that name should be present on the label, even if the medicine is available as a proprietary product. If the prescribed medication has several ingredients but no official or proprietary name, the medication is labelled by its pharmaceutical form, e.g., the mixture, the ointment, the lotion, etc. Preparation of **Labels for Dispensed Medicines**

Strength of the Medicine: The medication strength should be on the label if preparations are available in different strength. If an official preparation has its strength mentioned in the monograph, the official publication can be referred on the label, e.g., Calamine Lotion I. P., Sulphur Ointment I.P., Tannic Acid Glycerine I.P., etc. However, if the strength of an official preparation is not stated in the monograph, then its strength should be included in the label, e.g., Chloramphenicol Oral Suspension I.P., Chlorohexidine Cream I.P., and Aminophylline Suppositories.

Quantity in the Container: The total quantity of the medication dispensed in the container should be given on the label. If more than one container with the same medicine is dispensed, the amount in each container should be mentioned on the label.

Preparation of Labels for Dispensed Medicines

Storage Conditions and Shelf-Life of the Product: The pharmacists should provide the following guidelines on the label regarding the storage conditions: Temperature: There are many products that need to be stored in a cool place below 15°C temperature. High temperature can damage pessaries and suppositories that are designed to melt at body temperature. Immunological products and insulin injections should be stored between 2-8°C temperatures. Formaldehyde should be stored in a moderately warm place.

Humidity: The solid unit dosage forms that need to be protected from moisture should be dispensed in air - and moisture-proof containers. The patients should be guided to replace the cap after every use. Powdered dosage forms should be stored in a dry place. **Light:** The light -sensitive products should be stored in amber- coloured containers, which should be further stored in cardboard boxes. Even the light - resistant containers should not be exposed to Preparation of Labels for Dispensed Medicines

Instructions to the Patient: The following clear and complete instructions should be provided on the label for the patients regarding the use of medication:

Directions: The prescriber writes in the prescription the directions for use including the dose, frequency, timing, and route of the drug administration.

Shaking of the Bottle: Emulsions, suspensions, and aerosols for internal or external use should be shaken well before use to make the preparation homogeneous. Thus, this instruction should be provided on the label of such preparations to ensure dosage accuracy. Take with Water: Mixtures that can cause gastrointestinal irritation or mixtures for geriatrics having a dose of 10ml or more should be diluted with water before administration. Medicines for paediatrics having a dose of 5ml are not diluted; however, the preparations causing irritation need to be diluted.

Preparation of Labels for Dispensed Medicines

Cautionary and Advisory Labels To make the patients take their medicine in a safe and effective manner, they should be provided with essential information.

For External Use Only: This label should be applied on the containers of liquid preparations and all semi -solid and solid medicinal products, like gels, ointments, creams, pastes, and dusting powders, to be used externally.

Not to be Taken: This label should be applied on preparations not meant for oral intake or topical use. It is used for preparations meant for internal use, e.g., medicines for rectal, vaginal or nasal application. The labels, „For nasal use only", „For rectal use only", or „For vaginal use only", is preferred over „For external use only".

Warning: May cause drowsiness. If affected, do not drive or operate machinery, avoid alcoholic drink.

Drowsiness Warning: Some medicines can cause drowsiness, dizziness, blurred vision, or may impair the ability to drive or operate machinery safely. The patients should be warned about these indications while the medicines are being dispensed. The following instructions should be written on the Warning: May cause drowsiness. If affected, do not drive or operate machinery, avoid alcoholic drink.

Drugs to Ambulatory Patients: The terms "Outpatients" or "Ambulatory patients" refers to the patients not admitted in the hospitals. In the modern era the ambulatory care or out patients setting has taken special important interest among the health care professionals. Labeling requirements for drugs dispensed to ambulatory patients (out-patients) Labels must contain: Name, address and telephone of the dispenser Full name of the patient Name of the drug, strength, and amount dispensed Directions to the patient regarding how to use the drug Name of the prescribing practitioner Name or initials of dispensing individual and date dispensed DEA caution labels and/or patient ancillary labels for safe use Pharmacy's identifying serial number will be affixed to containers of unit of use packaged drugs issued by the pharmacy, applies only to drugs dispensed from an outpatient pharmacy. All drugs dispensed to outpatients will be packaged to conform to the Poison Prevention Packaging Act PPPA (PL 91-601), December 30, 1970. **Categories of ambulatory patients:** Emergency care, referral or tertiary care and primary care

HOSPITAL FORMULARY

Formulary is an official or authorized publication of an approved list of medicines. The hospital formulary is a list of pharmaceutical agents with its important information which reflects the current clinical views of the medical staff.

Hospital formulary is the list of the medicines including, Ancillary information related to toxicity, Unwanted side effects, Beneficial effects of some drugs which are considered most useful and safe in patient-care by a hospital.

It is a method whereby the medical staff of a hospital with the help of **Pharmacy and Therapeutic committee (PTC)**, selects and evaluate medical agents and their dosage form which are considered to be most useful in the patient care.

It provides the information for procuring, prescribing, dispensing and administering of drugs under non- proprietary or proprietary (brands) names in instances where drugs have both names.

Primary objectives are – Information on drug, Information on hospital policies & procedures, Special information.

<u>Advantages of hospital</u> **formulary** It provides the practitioner with approved and efficacious medicines to treat disease.

It reduces the inventory cost of the drugs.

It regulates the number of medicines by improving the procurement and inventory management.

It improves the quality assurance and easier dispensing.

It gives medicine information to resident staff, nurses and students

It removes the irrational combinations of drugs and also improves adverse drug reaction management. Disadvantages

The physician is deprived of prescribing drugs of his choice.

It may lead to purchase of drugs which are inferior in quality, in case of no involvement of the pharmacist in the preparation of formulary

Contents of Hospital Formulary PTC outline the purpose, organization function and scope of the hospital formulary system, it should adopt the principle as per the need of particular hospital.

The objectives of a formulary are to control use of drugs and provide proper and useful information to the prescribers.

In accordance with the objectives, the formulary should consist of three main parts:

A. Information on Drug products

B. Information on hospital policies & procedures

C. Special information

A. Information on Drug products This section is heart of formulary and consist of descriptive entries for each item to facilitate its use– Entries in formulary such as generic name of basic drugs; common name (Brand name); dosage form, strength, packaging; dose for various age group; route of administration; cost.

Drug product listing –Indexing by 2 ways

Generic name/brand name,

Therapeutic or pharmacological index

B. Information on hospital policies and Procedures Drug usage and restriction on drug use

Description of PTC including member responsibility.

Hospital regulations regarding prescribing, dispensing; administration of drug; drug orders; investigational drug policy; rules for Medical Representatives, emergency drug products etc.

Pharmacy operation procedures such as services, outpatients' prescription, inpatient drug distribution, labelling, packaging etc

Information on how to use formulary

C. Special information Useful to hospital staff and should be readily available.

It includes- Hospital approved abbreviations

Equivalent dosages of similar drugs

Guidelines for calculating pediatric dosages

 List of sugar free drugs Metric conversion tables

Poison control information

Table of drug interaction

GUIDLINE FOR HOSPITAL FORMULARY

a) b) c) d) The governing body of the hospital shall appoint a pharmacy and therapeutic committee composed of physician and pharmacist which will prepare the hospital formulary system.

b) The medical staff in the governing body shall sponsor and outline the purpose,organisation function and scope of the hospital formulary system. it should adopt the principle as per the need of particular hospital.

c) The pharmacy and therapeutic committee shall develop policy and procedure governing the hospital formulary and the medical staff shall adopt these policies and procedures subject to administrative approval

d) The policy and procedures shall afford guidance in the appraisal, selection, procurement, storage, distribution, use, safety procedures and other matter relating to drug in the hospital and shall be published in the hospital's formulary or other media available to the member of medical staff.

e) To ensure the maintenance of the responsibility and procreative of the physician in the exercise of his professional judgment.

f) The medical staff shall adopt the policy formula, and procedure for including drugs in the formulary by their non-proprietary names even though proprietary names even though proprietary names continue to being use in the hospital physicians. he may be encouraged to prescribe drug under their non-proprietary names, although nomenclature used in entirely a matter of individual practisner's discretion.

g) In the absence of written policies approved by the medical staff related to the operation

h) The hospital shall make it certain that the nursing personnel are informed in writing though its system of news of communication that there exits the formulary system in the hospital and the procedure governing its operations

i) In the formulation of policies and procedure the term substitute or substitution should be avoid since this term have been used to imply the unauthorized dispensing of entirely different drug, neither of which takes place under a properly operated hospital formulary system.

j) It shall be made known to the medical staff about the changes in the working in the hospital formulary system or in the content of the hospital system.

k) Provision shall be made for the appraisal of the member of the medical staff for the use of the drug not include in the formulary or the investigational drugs.

l) The pharmacist with the advice and guidance of the pharmacy and therapeutic committee, shall ascertain the quantity and source of supply of all drugs, chemical, biological and pharmaceutical preparation used for diagnosis and treatment of patient.

m) The labelling of drug and medicine container with non-proprietary name of the content always should be proper. The use of proprietary name other than that describing the actual content is not correct and proper if it is used in a manner that can be taken as description of the content.

Preparation of Hospital Formulary

Preparation of a hospital formulary is a principal responsibility of the pharmacy and therapeutic committee. How ever it is also rests primarily on the chief pharmacist service etc.

The committee is free to make necessary decisions, regarding the material to be included in the formulary and pharmacist undertaken the production of the formulary that is compiling and printing etc.

Irrespective of the decision arrived at in respect of above. it will be necessary to formulate a series of rules of guidelines which the committee may to evaluate drugs for admission to the formulary or the list of drugs.

If it is decided that the publication is to be a formulary, a decision must be reached as to the possible contents other than the section on various therapeutic agents.

i) Section on prescription writing.

ii) Section governing the use of drug.

iii) Section on diagnostic reagent and normal pathological investigational reagent etc.

iv) Section on pharmaceutical classification etc which are good guidelines for pharmacist and nurses.

v) Poision and their antidote.

vi) Posological tablet.

vii) Other useful data and feature e.g. tablet of metric weight and measure and their equivalent of apothecary" and household measures, calculation and dosages for various age group especially of children.

viii) It should also be decided at the outset, as what short of format should the formulary adopt and how should be its

a) size

b) printed or cyclostyled

C) whether lose leaf or bound, the advantage of the former is that addiction and deletion of pages of various section or main body of the drug list are possible.

Composition-

1. Title page

2. Names & titles of the members of the PTC

3. Table of contents

4. Information on hospital policies & procedures concerning drugs

5. Products accepted for use at hospital

6. Appendix

Contents:

List of abbreviations, List of drugs used in the formulary

Basic information on each drug: Efficacy; Safety profile of; Interaction profile; Adverse effects; Pharmacokinetic profile; Availability of the item; Available dosage form; Cost; Acceptability to patients.

Supplementary information on each drug: Storage guidelines; Labelling information; Brand names and prices; Patient counselling information.

Prescription guidelines: Principles of prescription writing; Reporting of ADR; Prevention of ADR.

General drug advice: Special situations like pregnancy, breast feeding, liver/kidney diseases; Poisoning information and antidotes; Miscellaneous information: Children's dose; diagnostic aids.

Differentiation of hospital formulary and drug list:

Hospital Formulary

Listing of drugs by their generic names followed by information on strength, form, posology, toxicology, use & recommended quantity to be dispensed.

Prepared locally by its own clinical staff.

Information provided is subject to local needs and desires.

Published in convenient size

Addition or deletion of drug with greater frequency

Drug List

Generic names followed by data on strength & form.

Prepared by country's outstanding clinicians, pharmacologists and pharmacists.

According to their pharmacological properties.

Size is big

Addition or deletion of drug with lesser frequency

Revision of Hospital Formulary

The revision of any drug to the formulary is a complex decision.

The PTC holds meetings to discuss about the revision of the formulary and the specialized expert are invite

The annual revision is necessary because of the changes in the drug products, removal of certain drugs from the market and changes in the hospital policies.

All steps prior to the addition or deletion of a drug must be reported to the medical staff.

It is done by attaching the supplement sheets at the back of the formulary or by using different colour for the cover of each edition

During revision, cost effectiveness and cost benefit analysis methods are used

Criteria for addition or deletion of drugs

The subject drug must be present in the Pharmacopoeia or National Formulary.

The drugs of established therapeutic efficacy can only be added to the formulary

The subject drug product should receive approval for its clinical value by the local or specialized physicians

The drug product is to be manufactured by a licensed company with a good record.

The preparation of known composition can only be added to the formulary.

No preparation of secrete composition will be consider

No product of multiple ingredients shall be admitted if he same therapeutic effect can be achieved

THERAPEUTIC DRUG MONITORING

Therapeutic drug monitoring: TDM refers to the measurement and interpretation of principally blood or plasma drug concentration measurements with the purpose of optimizing a patient's drug therapy and clinical outcome while minimizing the risk of drug induced toxicity.

(TDM) refers to the measurement of drug concentrations in biological fluids with the purpose of optimising a patient's drug therapy. During administration of a dosage regimen, the concentration should be maintained within the therapeutic window.

TDM refers to the tool utilised to individualise dosage regimen by maintaining plasma or blood drug concentrations within the therapeutic range.

Therapeutic Range/ Therapeutic Window: The therapeutic range/ therapeutic window is the concentration range of drug in plasma where the drug has been shown to be efficacious without causing toxic effects in most people.

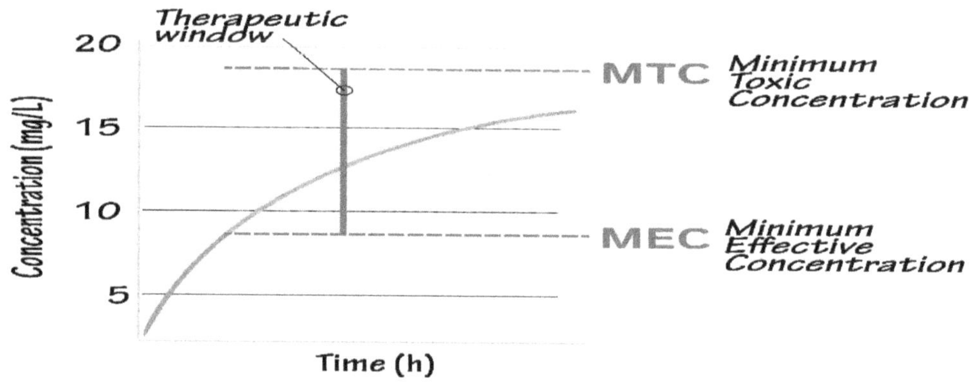

THERAPEUTIC WINDOW
Range between the minimum toxic concentration (MTC) and the minimum effective concentration (MEC).

Need for TDM

1. Drugs which have narrow therapeutic index
2. Drugs for which small changes in the concentration of the drug in plasma are likely to exhibit large changes in drug response (should exhibit non-linear kinetics)
3. Drugs which exhibit poor and erratic absorption
4. Drugs which exhibit relatively wider inter-individual variation in drug metabolism
5. Patient exhibiting the signs and symptoms of toxicity (Theophylline intake and persistent nausea
6. To minimize the risk of toxicity

7. To identify the poison and to determine the severity

8. 8. Drugs where signs of over dosage or under dosage are difficult to distinguish.

9. Drugs which are administered in the presence of gastrointestinal, hepatic or renal disease

10. When patients are receiving multiple drug therapy.

DRUGS THAT ARE NOT SUITABLE FOR TDM

1) Drugs having wide therapeutic index, NSAIDS

2) Toxicity is not a realistic concern (Penicillin)

3) Effects can be measured using functional laboratory tests (Anticoagulants), Oral Antidiabetics, anti-Hypertensives etc.

4) Plasma concentration not predictably related to effects (Anticoagulants)

5) Effect of the relationship remains undefined (Antidepressants)

6) Hit and run drugs: Omeprazole, MAO inhibitors

NARROW THERAPEUTIC DRUGS

Bronchodilators: Theophylline

Antibiotics – Aminoglycosides - Gentamicin, Amikacin – Others – Vancomycin

Immunosuppressants: Cyclosporine

Anticancer: Methotrexate

Antiepileptics: Phenobarbital, Phenytoin, Valproate

Cardiac Drugs: Digoxin, Procainamide, Lidocaine

Psychoactive Drugs: Lithium

Factors affecting TDM

1. Patient demographics Age, sex and lean body weight are particularly important for renally cleared drugs as knowledge of these allows calculation of creatinine clearance.

2. Patient Compliance If the concentration of the drug is lower than expected, the possibility of non-compliance should be considered before a dose increase is recommended.

3. Individuals capacity to absorb/distribute/metabolize/excrete the drug

    Absorption: The rate of absorption and extent of absorption are dependent on various factors such as:

    Drug formulation

    Manufacturer

    Route of administration

    Intra-individual variations

    Another aspect of absorption is bioavailability.

This is the fraction of the administered dose that reaches the systemic circulation. Bioavailability is 100% for IV injection.

4. **Distribution:** (Vd) = dose/plasma concentration The absolute bioavailability of a drug. For example if a drug has a half life of four hours, four hours after the initial dose, 50% of the drug will be removed. Eight hours after the initial dose, half of the remaining drug (25% of total) will be removed, for a total of 75% having been removed at that time, and so on. Half-life information is used to determine the correct drug dose required to attain the desired therapeutic range

5. **Metabolism:** In addition, drug metabolites can be either protein bound (inactive) or free (active). The drug dosage will depend on how the drug metabolizes. Factors that impact drug metabolism includes genetics, environment, nutrition,drug interaction and age.

6. **Excretion:** Drug excretion from the body occurs through the kidneys, or fluids excreted through the lungs, GI or skin. Renal dysfunction reduces drug clearance and may contribute to drug accumulation and increased risk of adverse drug effects.

7. **Some other causes:** Age: In general, drugs metabolized more slowly in foetal, neonatal, and geriatric populations.

   Physical properties of the drug (hydrophobicity, pKa, solubility)If the drug is administered in a fed or fasted state Gastric emptying rate

8. **Enzyme induction/inhibition by other drugs/foods:-**

   Enzyme induction (increase rate of metabolism). e.g. Phenytoin, barbiturates, carbamazepine, glutethimide, primidone, rifampicin induces CYP1A2, CYP2C9, CYP2C19 and CYP3A4, which is involved in a drug's metabolism may reduce the drug's activity.

   Enzyme inhibition (decrease rate of metabolism), resulting in ↑ drug activity, e.g. Protease inhibitors, Nitrogen mustard, Mtx, Sildenafil Citrate.

9. Concomitant disease, Tropical disease and nutritional deficiencies This includes diseases highly prevalent in developing countries such as Infections, Diarrhoea, Worm infestations, Tuberculosis, Nutritional deficiencies, plus a higher proportion of patients with diabetes and AIDS

10. **Alternative system of medicine** India is unique in having at least three systems of medicine coexisting with 'western' medicine (Allopathy); Ayurveda, Homeopathy and Unani. A patient with a history of generalized tonic-clonic (GTC) seizures, well

controlled and with plasma phenytoin levels within the therapeutic range, presented with sudden loss of seizure control.

11. **Alcohol & Tobacco use** Chronic use of alcohol has been shown to cause non-specific hepatic microsomal enzyme induction, resulting in increased clearance and decreased serum concentrations of hepatically cleared drugs. Cigarette smoking increases the hepatic clearance of theophylline and patients who have recently stopped smoking may have unexpectedly high theophylline concentrations.

12. **Medication or sampling errors:** In cases where the TDM result is incompatible with drug administration records, the possibility of a medication or sampling error should be considered. For Example, the drug may have been given to the wrong patient, or blood may have been mistakenly drawn from a patient in a neighboring bed.

13. **Laboratory errors:** If a laboratory error is suspected, the laboratory should be contacted and asked to repeat the assay. Alternatively, a new blood sample can be drawn and sent to a different laboratory for assay.

14. **Cost effectiveness:** Rapid and cost-effective measurement of most drugs for which TDM is indicated can be achieved using commercial kits run on automated analysers using a number of different methodologies including fluorescence polarisation immunoassay.

15. **Testing Methodologies** In HPLC liquid containing sample is injected at one end of the column. high pressure is used to overcome resistance to flow as liquid flows some molecule move faster than others due to diff in solubility.

The exact time for each molecule to flow through the column is measured by detector. The retention time is calculated. An internal standard compound similar in structure to the specimen to be analyzed is also run through the column. By comparing retention time of sample and standard molecule can be identified. Concentration of drug can also be determined that peak produce during run.

INDIAN SENARIO OF TDM

The current population of India is 1,384,715,664 as of Friday, November 6, 2020, based on World meter elaboration of the latest United Nations data. India 2020 population is estimated at 1,380,004,385 people at midyear according to UN data. India population is equivalent to 17.7% of the total world population. India ranks number 2 in the list of countries (and dependencies) by population.

In such a populated country it is very challenging for the health care providers to fulfill the services.

Rural areas in India have a shortage of medical professionals. 74% of doctors are in urban areas that serve the other 28% of the population. This is a major issue for rural access to healthcare.

In such a condition TDM will be somewhere unheared in India.

Challenges In India to Perform Tdm.

Lack of health care providers

Scientific accuracy of the drug assay

Over population

Poverty in india

Lack of facilities and equipments in hospitals

Expensive tdm process

No recruitment of tdm process team in indian hospitals.

Clinical Challenges in Therapeutic Drug Monitoring

Clinical Challenges in Therapeutic Drug Monitoring:

Special Populations, Physiological Conditions and Pharmacogenomics focuses on critical issues in therapeutic drug monitoring including special requirements of therapeutic drug monitoring important to special populations (infants and children, pregnant women, elderly patients, and obese patients).

Difficult to identify the special population in Indian populations.

Some Drugs to Which We Perform Tdm

1. Antiepileptic drugs: Phenytoin, phenobarbitone, benzodiazepines, carbamazepine, valproic acid and ethosuximide

2. Antimicrobial agents: Aminoglycoside

3. Antineoplastics: Methotrexate, Busulfan, 6-Mercaptopurine

4. Cardioactive Drugs: Amiodarone, digoxin, digitoxin, disopyramide, lignocaine, procainamide, propranolol and quinidine

5. Immunosuppressants: Cyclosporine, Tacrolimus, Sirolimus

6. Antidepressants: Lithium and tricyclic antidepressants

7. Bronchodilators: Theophylline, Caffeine

THERAPEUTIC DRUG MONITORING (TDM) REQUEST FORM

PATIENT PROFILE

Name	:		Ward / Unit	:		RN/IC	:
Age	:	years	Sex	: Male / Female		Race	:
Weight (kg)	:		Height (cm)	:		DOA	:

CLINICAL SUMMARY AND DIAGNOSIS

PATIENT CONDITION			INDICATION FOR REQUEST	
□ Oedema	□ Smoker	□ Dehydration	□ Therapeutic Monitoring	□ Poor Response
□ Dialysis	□ Burn	□ Liver Disease	□ Suspected Toxicity	□ Non Compliance

LATEST LAB RESULT / CONCURRENT MEDICATION

	Date	Result
Blood Urea		
Na^+ / K^+		
Creatinine		
Albumin		

Drug Analysis Tick [V] where Appropriate	Present Dose Regimen	Date Started	Last Dose	Time Pre-sampling	Dose Given	Post Given
Acetaminophen						
Amikacin						
Digoxin						
Carbamazepin						
Gentamicin						
Phenobarbitone						
Phenytoin						
Salicylate						
Theophylline						
Valproic Acid						
Vancomycin						
Cyclosporin						

Refer to TDM Serum Sample Guide

For injectable drug being analysed :

Infusion rate :

Duration of Infusion :

____
Doctor's Signature   Name & Stamp   Date

Drug Analysis	Result	Normal Therapeutic Range	Pharmacokinetic Profiles		Date Received:
			K	:	
			$T_{1/2}$	:	Time Received:
			V_d	:	Test Done :
			Cr_{CL}	:	Initials :

Pharmacist's Assessment and Recommendation:

MEDICATION ADHERENCE

Medication Adherence: The patient's conformance with the provider's recommendation with respect to timing, dosage and frequency of medication-taking during the prescribed length of time. It is a factor that determines the therapeutic out comes, in a patient suffering from chronic illness/diseases. Compliance: How well the patient follows the instruction of when and how to take the medication Persistence: Duration of time patient takes medication, from initiation to discontinuation of therapy.

Causes of Medication Non-Adherence

Socio-economic

Poor socioeconomic status, illiteracy, unemployment

Lack of family or social support

Lack of financial resources

Busy work schedules

High cost of medication

Health care system related

Relationship of doctor-patient

Poor or lack of proper communication regarding the beneficial effect of taking medication, instructions for use and side effects

Poor medication distribution

Therapy related

Complexity of medical regimens, duration of treatments

Lack of immediate benefit of therapy and treatment interferes with lifestyle

Condition related

Severity of symptoms (chronic illness requires long term drugs administration OR few or no symptoms)

Patient related

Impairments such as visual, hearing and cognitive impairments and swallowing problems Lack of motivation, apprehension about possible adverse side effects

Stress, anxiety

Pharmacists Role in Medication Adherence

Pharmacists can improve medication adherence because they can actually show the medication to the patient and relate any information to the medication itself.

Educate patients regarding medication adherence

Pharmacists can impart the information that patients need to know such as-

Name and purpose of the drug,

When and how to take the medication,

Possible side effects, Precautions, Interaction with food or other drugs,

Duration of therapy,

Action to take if a dose is missed etc.

A pharmacist can advise to prescribers on the simplification of drug regimens and reinforcing factors which may contribute towards medication non- adherence.

A pharmacists can assess the patient's knowledge of their drug therapy and usual medication habits

The pharmacists can also assess the patient's ability to comprehend and recall information, and if an adverse drug reaction may discourage medication adherence.

Strategies to improve the pharmacist-patient relationship:

Be friendly and approachable to the patient. ☐ Improve communication skills.

Take into account the spiritual and psychological needs of the patient.

Improving patient education.

Give clear explanation.

Check the patient understanding.

Simplify the therapeutic regimes.

Monitor the side effects.

Monitor the beneficial effects.

Speak the same language of patient.

Involvement of patient treatment discussion.

Monitoring of Medication Adherence

Assessment, quantification, measurement and evaluation of adherence

Direct and Indirect methods

The direct measurement includes –

Drug monitoring

Detection of the drug or its metabolites in biological fluid

Direct observation therapy

Most accurate methods of adherence measurement but are expensive

The Indirect measurement includes –

Self-reports,

Pill counts,

Rates of prescription refills,

Assessment of the patient's clinical response

Measurement of physiologic markers as well as patient diaries

Direct Measurement: -

Home finger prick sampling

Biological markers

Directly observed therapy

Indirect Measurements: -

Self-report measures (using questionnaires)

Morisky's medication adherence scale

Medical outcome adherence study scale

Brief Adherence Rating Scale

Electronic Adherence monitoring

Factors Affecting Medication Adherence

Patient related factors

Income

Literacy

Age of patient

Gender

Knowledge of disease

Severity of disease

Marital status

Attitude for treatment

Efficiency of therapy

Therapeutic Regimen

Anxiety

Anger

ADR

Disability

Unable to swallow

Stress

Fear of ADR/ Dependence

Social And Economic Factor

Busy schedule o Less access to health facility

Low access to Pharmacy

Less health literacy

Lack of family and social support

Cultural belief about disease

Disease related factor

Less symptoms of severity

No symptom or disappearance of symptom

Psychological diseases

Health care provider related factors

Relationship with provider

Poor communication

Poor understanding

Busy schedule

Waiting period

      Lack of continuous care

      Lack of Knowledge

      Missing appointments

Therapy related factors

Number of doses

Duration of therapy

Frequent changes in drugs

Lack of Immediate relief

ADR/Side effect

Monitoring of Patient Medication Adherence

Direct method

Directly observe the treatment

Measure the concentration of drug in blood or metabolite in urine Drawback

Expensive

Patient hide drug in mouth

Altered metabolism

Indirect method

Count the medicine (Tablet/Capsule)

Questionnaires for patients

Refill rates of Prescription

Measure Pharmacological response

Electronic medication monitors

Drawbacks

Expensive

Patient may lie

Response may be change due to various factors

Monitoring of Patient Medication Adherence

Medication event Monitoring system

Easy method

It records date and time of medication intake

Bottles are fitted with microprocessor embedded technology in cap

Drawback

Patient may manipulate the regimen (Open bottle so many times, may take excess dose)

Expensive

Inaccurate

PATIENT MEDICATION HISTORY INTERVIEW

Medication history is a part of pharmaceutical consultation that identifies and document allergies or other serious adverse medication events as well as information about how medicines are taken currently and have been taken in the past. • Starting point for medication reconciliation and medication review • Part of medical history which focuses on medication therapy.

Goals of Medication History

To gain information on ☐Prescription and nonprescription medications

Perceived benefit or adverse effects of the therapy

Medication allergy/intolerance • Identification of potential medication problems

To develop more through assessment and pharmaceutical care plan.

Better patient outcomes

Need of Medication History Interview

Preventing prescription errors and consequent risk to patients.

 Useful in detecting drug –related pathology or changes in clinical signs that may be the result of drug therapy.

It should encompass all currently and recently prescribed drugs, previous adverse drug reactions including herbal or alternative medicines and adherence to therapy for better care plan.

The following information is commonly recorded:

1. Currently or recently prescribed medicines

2. OTC medication

3. Vaccinations

4. Alternative or traditional remedies

 5. Description of reactions and allergies to medicine

6. Medicines found to be ineffective

7. Adherence to past treatment and use of adherence aids

Types of Data Collection

Subjective:

Information provided by the patient

Cannot confirmed/observed/measured

Other measure to validate it

Objective:

Measurable and observed

 Not influenced by the opinion/perception of the patient

Sources of Patient Data:

Patient interview

Medical records

Pharmacy dispensing records

Health care providers

Care giver/family members

Components of Patient Drug History

1) Demographic and patient financial insurance information

2) Medication allergies and intolerance

3) Immunizations

4) Medications

5) Additional home monitoring and compliance aids

6) Barriers to compliance

7) Additional information for patient history:

- Social history

- Acute/chronic medical problems

Aspects of medication use obtained from medication history interview

History of previous allergies/ADR

Perceived efficacy

Perceived side effects

Adherence to medication

Medication administration techniques

Specific problems related to medicine use

Possibility of pregnancy in women of child bearing age.

Steps involved in Medication History Interview

1) Patient Selection

2) Self Preparation

3) Privacy and confidentiality

4) Purpose of interview

5) Conduct interview

6) Conclusion

7) Document and follow-up

1) Patient Selection

Ideally all Patient

If not, possible priority should be given to those who are more likely to get benefit.

Eg: Patient with polypharmacy, Multiple and chronic diseases.

Certain diseases it is not possible to take medication history interview like psychiatric disorders, impaired cognition etc.

Consider family members or relatives.

2) Self Preparation

Collect all the relevant data including co- morbid conditions

Make use of various sources of data

Provisional list of medications can be made through medical notes

Preparation of list of questions can be helpful

3) Privacy and Confidentiality

Consider privacy and confidentiality of the patient

Hospital setting – difficult to maintain because interviews are taken at bedside

Patient unable to communicate – family members can be involved

Must maintain confidentiality of the data except for exchange of information with other health care professionals.

4) Purpose of interview

Introduce him/herself and explain the purpose of interview

Possible benefits should also be explained

Respect patient right to decline the interview

5) Conduct Interview

Use proper communication skills during interview

Where possible ask open ended questions

Close ended questions may be useful to confirm details

All the questions asked appropriately

6) Conclusion

Check whether all important and relevant details obtained

Ask patient if he/she has any questions relating to the medications.

7) Documentation and follow up

All information should be documented

Documented medications should be compared with the information obtained from health care professionals for any discrepancies.

If any discrepancies – informed to the concerned physician

Documented information will be helpful for ongoing pharmaceutical care

Medication History Interview form

Demographic Data :

Patient's Name	Male/Female
Consultant	Ward
Admission Date	Interview Date

1 <u>PRESCRIBED MEDICATION</u> -(What medicines are you having at the moment?)

A)Record here what the patient says, noting any anomalies with their current prescription

B)Other drugs prescribed previously(with date if possible) - what have you had in the past?

2 <u>NON PRESCRIBED MEDICATION</u> -Do you take anything that you buy from a shop without a prescription-chemist, health food stores, super market?

A)Currently being used

B)Used previously(with dates if possible)

3 <u>SOCIAL DRUGS</u> – Ask what and how much/many per week?

A)Smoking
B)Alcohol
C)Illicit Drugs

4 Response to Drug Therapy -

A)Do you think your current medication is benefiting you?
If yes, how?

If no, why?

COMMUNITY PHARMACY MANAGEMENT

The Community Pharmacy Medicines Management (CPMM) is a unique concept that aims to introduce a structured intervention process among the community pharmacist, the patent, and the general practitioner.

The whole study is based on Randomised Controlled Trial (RCT).

The managerial activities that involve planning, decision-making, organising, staffing, directing, and controlling are useful in the management of a setting.

The management functions generally are defined as all the acts involved in the organisation and functioning of the elements of an enterprise for economic benefits.

Man, money, material, and equipment are brought together in a proper relationship to achieve the objectives and goals that management has decoded.

Success of a community pharmacy depends on three factors, i.e., its location (site), proper layout, and design.

Objectives

The **primary objectives** of the CPMM are to:

Study and compare the number of patients receiving proper treatment that abide by the currently available evidences and guidelines, between intervention and control groups at baseline and follow-up.

Describe the changes occurring in health status of a patient after the intervention as defined by standard measures, under both general and specific conditions.

Perform an economic evaluation of the medicines management intervention (estimating the changes occurring in drug prices).

The **secondary objectives** of the CPMM are to:

Describe the opinions of the stakeholders (patients, physicians, community pharmacists, and hospital staff) on medicine management before and after its introduction.

Describe the importance of OTC (Over the Counter) medicines in the overall patient management.

FINANCIAL REQUIREMENT

Financial planning is one of the most important steps taken by a community pharmacy. This step is generally taken right after the pharmacy inception and setting of vision and objectives of the drug store. A financial plan details out various activities to be carried out by the community pharmacy and resources available for achievement of the set objectives within stipulated time. Financial planning is concerned with the determination of strategic objectives of the community pharmacy and the means to achieve them.

Functions of Financial Planning

Analysing the business environment for drug store,

Designing business objectives and goals for drug store,

Identification of resources required for the achievement of set business goals,

Detailed analysis and quantification of medical resources,

Creating budgets to determine total costs involved, and

Critically analysing the budget for potential issue.

Objectives of Financial Planning

Proper Fund Flow: The main objective of a financial plan is to ensure that pharmacy does not suffer due to paucity of funds. There should be proper flow of funds which optimises pharmacy business operation profitability.

Minimise Risk and Cost: A financial plan of a community pharmacy seeks to minimise costs and ensure that there will be minimum risk related to the procurement and use of funds.

Easy to Understand: A financial plan of a community pharmacy should be able to make all the concerned parties understand the terms and conditions in the simplest possible manner.

Flexible: A good financial plan in a community pharmacy must be flexible so that it can be adjusted to suit the requirements of change in circumstances.

Sound Liquidity: Another objective of a financial plan is to ensure that the community pharmacy is able to honour its commitment as and when they arise. Thus, the community pharmacy should design financial plan considering both the growth as well as declining stages of business.

Proper Use of Funds: A financial plan not only ensures the availability of funds according to the requirements but also makes sure that the funds are not lying idle.

Practice Economy: A financial plan seeks to obtain funds at the least possible cost. A firm needs to set up proper plan to obtain funds in such manner.

Financial Planning in Community Pharmacy

The financial section in a business plan of a community pharmacy gives a financial view of the services being offered. The financial plan of a community pharmacy represents the sources or services through which the pharmacists are expecting to generate revenues,

e.g., consulting fees, sale of medicines, estimated expenses including salary of staff, marketing cost, rent, utilities, supplies, and equipment. The financial plan which is made should predict the break-even point of the services.

The financial plan of the community pharmacy helps in projecting revenue and expenses of the store. Based on the fluctuating demand of the medical products, the financial plan must consist of low, moderate and high estimates for revenue. Before developing the financial plan, the pharmacists must analyse the possible source of income and cost linked with the services that are offered.

The financial plan of a community pharmacy must include the following statements:

• **Income and Expense Statements:** These statements are those in which the profit and loss of the community pharmacy is shown after a specific time period, i.e., annually.

• **Balance Sheet:** This shows the financial position of the community pharmacy in the form of asset and liability on a specific date.

• **Cash Flow Statement:** This statement represents the movement of money into the business or out of the community pharmacy via operating, financing and investing activities.

Projections of Financial Plan in Community Pharmacy

Projecting Revenue: This revenue is calculated taking into consideration the income from product sale and fee -based services. Example of the product sale is revenue generated from the sale of non prescribed medicines and other OTC products. It may also include sale of non-pharmacologic product such as device used to measure hypertension or diabetes, other health care products, etc. The other source of revenue is fee-based compensation. The financial plan should contain proposed fees and the rationale for setting them if the primary market is of cash -paying patients. It should also contain structure of the fees according to the services.

Projecting Expenses: These expenses means that the financial plan of a community pharmacy must include the expected expenses, which will incur in the initial stage or in the ongoing pharmacy business. Projecting expenses in advance will ensure that the pharmacy has sufficient cash flow and adequate availability of funds in their reserve until the services exceed the break-even point.

Some of the projected expenses are as follows:

Start-up Cost: This includes the cost of training and change in the plan of the pharmacy. Start -up cost also includes the cost of replacing an old technology with the new one.

Fixed Cost: This is the cost that remain s constant throughout even with the increase or decrease in the quantity of medical goods produced, e.g., salary, insurance premium, building rent, etc.

Variable Cost: This is the cost that keeps on changing with the change in the level of production of pharmaceutical products. If the production increase s, the variable cost increases and vice-versa.

MATERIAL REQUIREMENT

Stocking

The drugs purchased from the market are stored in drug stores to continue a uniform supply of drugs to the patients. They are stored in containers, such as drums and boxes and on flexible racks, etc.

During their storage period, the medicines stored in a drug store should remain preserved. They should not get damaged by high temperature or exposure to sunlight. Drugs should be stored according to the prescribed conditions of their storage.

Objectives

Stocking has the following objectives:

The drugs can be easily located in the store.

The drugs and other items can be properly identified.

A supply of materials can be maintained.

Maximum utilisation of space can be done.

The use of materials handling equipment can be minimised.

Functions

Stocking has the following fucntions:

It enables speedy functioning, i.e., receiving, handling and quick issue of material.

It prevents the goods against damage and pilferage during the storage period.

It ensures uninterrupted supply of materials.

It enables physically stocking the goods and checking them routinely.

It allows maximum utilisation of the available space.

It provides economical service to the organisation.

It permits easy identification and location of the items.

Arrangement of Drugs in a Community Pharmacy

In a community pharmacy, the drugs should be arranged in the following ways:

According to Manufacturer: The drugs are arranged according to the name of manufacturer. For example, the drugs manufactured by Glaxo (India) Ltd. are kept in a separate cupboard, and so on.

According to Pharmacological Action: The drugs are arranged according to their pharmacological action.

MATERIAL REQUIREMENT

Arrangement of Drugs in a Community Pharmacy

According to Alphabetical Order: The drugs are arranged in alphabetical order. For example, drugs having initial letter "A" are placed in one row of the cupboard; the other drugs in the same manner are placed according to their first alphabet.

As per Old Stock and Date of Expiry: Drugs of old stock are placed in front row and those of fresh stock are placed in back rows so that the older stock is sold first.

According to Location of Stores for Stocking: The stores should be located in such an area where handling, transportation and movement of the material are minimum. If more than one plant is situated in the same area, one centralises store should be located to serve all production operations.

Centralised storing has the following advantages:

Less investment is required.

Minimum incidental expenses.

Small space is required for storage.

The administrative costs are reduced as less manpower is required.

More bargaining because products are purchased in bulk.

Centralised storing has the following disadvantages:

Materials handling operations are performed on a large scale.

Delaying in service occurs commonly.

Coding

In the process of coding, a code number or code symbol is assigned to a particular material for easy identification. Generally, the manufacturers, distributors and wholesalers have large stock in the stores, and in such conditions, it becomes very difficult to identify the items without a proper system. Therefore, a system of code numbers is evolved to facilitate easy allocation and identification of each material stored.

Advantages

Coding has the following advantages:

It helps in easy identification of stored drug items.

It allows grouping of the similar items together.

The ambiguity of materials can be avoided.

The detailed description of the materials is not needed repeatedly.

Duplication of items can be avoided.

It makes physical counting easy.

Physical inspection of the materials is easy.

Confidentiality of the items can be maintained with coding system.

Methods

Coding can be done by the following methods:

Alphabetical Order Method or Letter Code: In this method, the items are coded alphabetically. For example, capsules are coded as "C", tablets as "T", and so on.

Mnemonic Method: In this method, each item is coded by some specific letters. For example, "APC" is used to code aspirin, paracetamol and caffeine. The drawback of this system is that the items cannot be recognised without referring code index book.

Numerical or Sequence System Method: In this method, separate numbers are assigned to specific item s of store. This method is further divided into the following sub-systems:

Block System: In this system, the numbers are already fixed for a particular item. For example, number 10 -50 is used to code various types of tablets; number series 10.1, 10.2, 10.3, and 10.4, codes for antipyretic s, analgesics, anti- inflammatory, and decongestants, respectively.

Decimal System: In this system, the numbers are used for coding such that each digit represents the particular name under same heading. For example, if the code for tablet is 10, then 10.1 (paracetamol- antipyretic), 10.2 (analgin- analgesic).

Combination Method: In this method, combined form of mnemonic and numerical methods is used to code different items of the store. For example, code "CPC" is assigned to chloramphenicol capsules; code "PAT 11" is for paracetamol with analgin tablets. This m ethod is mostly used when a large number of items are in store.

Locating Coding: A large organisation has a large number of store rooms , and each room is divided in blocks and each block is identified by lateral and longitudinal block letter. Thus , an item is located by its warehouse number, block number, row number, rack number , shelf number , etc. Any item inside the store rooms can be located as follows:

Fixed Location: In this system, all the groups of items are given a fixed place inside the store accor ding to the supplier wise, item wise , and a s per the utility of the item.

Random Location: This is the most common system used for allocation of drug items in a store. It is followed in all kinds of retail shops but each group items are stored, in a particular shelf for its easy location.

Zonal Location: In this system, the available space is divided into different zones and each zone is assigned for different items. The zones can be named as bulk zone, reserve stock zone, spare part zone, and consumable item zone.

Staff Requirement

For running an organisation smoothly, it is necessary to identify and fill various job positions with people who can effectively perform the given tasks. This process is known as staffing and is performed by the management.

The eligibility for establishing and operating a community pharmacy is that the person should be a registered pharmacist by the State Pharmacy Council. A person who has qualified Diploma or has a Degree in Pharmacy and has completed a training for 650 hours in a medical store recognised by the State Pharmacy Council or a government hospital is eligible to be registered as a pharmacist. Training is not compulsory for candidates having a degree in pharmacy.

For running a wholesale drug store, experience in pharmaceutical selling or production is also needed along with Diploma or Degree certificate. A science graduate (B.Sc.) with 10 years' experience of medical representative can also open a wholesale drug store.

The following employees are involved in a wholesale drug store:

1) Administrative executives,

2) Office employees,

3) Warehouse employees,

4) Inventory employees, and

5) Salesmen.

Importance of Staffing

A healthy organisation can be established by the process of staffing in which the job performance and satisfaction of every employee is priority.

Staffing gives life to the organisation by providing a suitable person for every job. The effectiveness of direction and controlling also depends on staffing.

For an organisation, its employees are the most valuable strength, as their quality and skills determine the success and growth of the organisation.

INFRASTRUCTURE REQUIREMENT

The infrastructure of a good community pharmacy is mainly based on the following factors:

Site selection for community pharmacy,

Space layout for community pharmacy, and

Design of community pharmacy.

Selection of Site

Selection of a suitable site is the main objective of entrepreneurs for making their business successful. Site selection is done after taking the decision of opening a community pharmacy, getting required qualifications and experience, and achieving the business skill required for creating financial support.

Classification of Location

Geographic Location: Rural or Small Town, Urban Town or Big City

Functional Location: Suscipient Location, Interceptive Location, Generative Location

Factors Affecting Selection of Site for a Drug House

Physicians • Hospitals

Drug Store

Flow of Traffic: Parking

Near to Hotel, School, Cinema House, or Play Ground

Business Locality

Thickly Populated Residential Areas

Developing Areas

Special Services

Customers

Shopping Centres

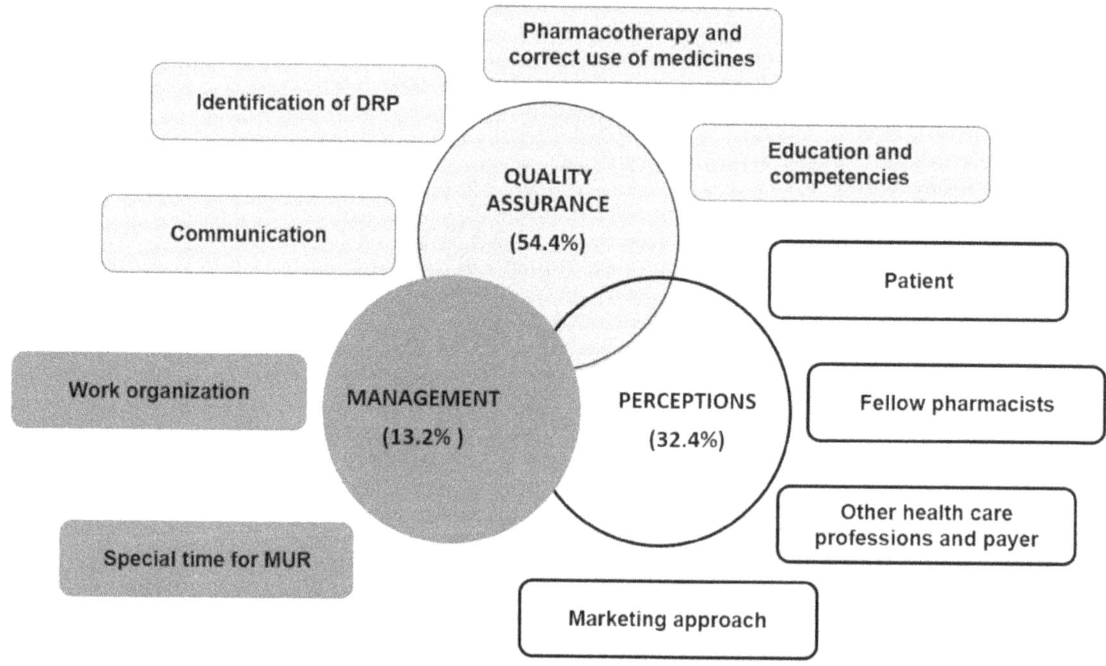

PHARMACY AND THERAPEUTIC COMMITTEE

The pharmacy and therapeutic committee are a policy framing and recommending body to the medical staff and the administration of hospital on matters related to therapeutic use of drugs. This committee is composed of physicians, pharmacists and other health professionals selected with the inclusion of medical staff.

Objective of the PTC:

The PTC has 3 major roles to play.

These are 1) Advisory 2) Educational 3) Drug safety and adverse drug monitoring

Advisory:

The committee recommends the adoption of policies or assists in the formulation of broad professional policies regarding evaluation, selection and therapeutic use of drugs in the hospital.

The committee serves in an advisory capacity to medical staff and hospital administration in all matters pertaining to the use of drugs, including the investigational drugs.

It makes recommendations concerning the drugs to be stocked in hospital patient care areas. The committee advises the pharmacy in implementation of effective drug distribution and control procedures.

Educational:

The committee recommends or assists in the formulation of functions, designed to meet the needs of professional staff like the physicians, nurses, pharmacist and other health care practitioners, for the complete current knowledge of the matter related to the drugs and their use.

The committee evaluates the problems related to the distribution and administration of medications, including medication incident.

The committee develops and compiles a formulary of drugs and prescriptions of formulations accepted for use in the hospital.

The committee should minimise duplication of the same basic drug, drug safety, and cost. It establishes or plans suitable educational schemes for the hospital's professional staff on the matters related to the use of drugs.

Drug safety and adverse drug monitoring:

This function is assigned to or taken up by the PTC and it should be continuous scheme of exerting vigilance.

Composition of PTC:

Composition of PTC might vary from hospital to hospital. It may compose of:

1. At least three physicians from the medical staff

2. A pharmacist

3. A representative of the nursing staff and

4. An hospital administrator with his or her designated an ex-officio member of the committee one of the physicians may be appointed as the chairman of PTC. The pharmacist functions usually as the secretary and therefore, he is designated as the Secretary of the committee.

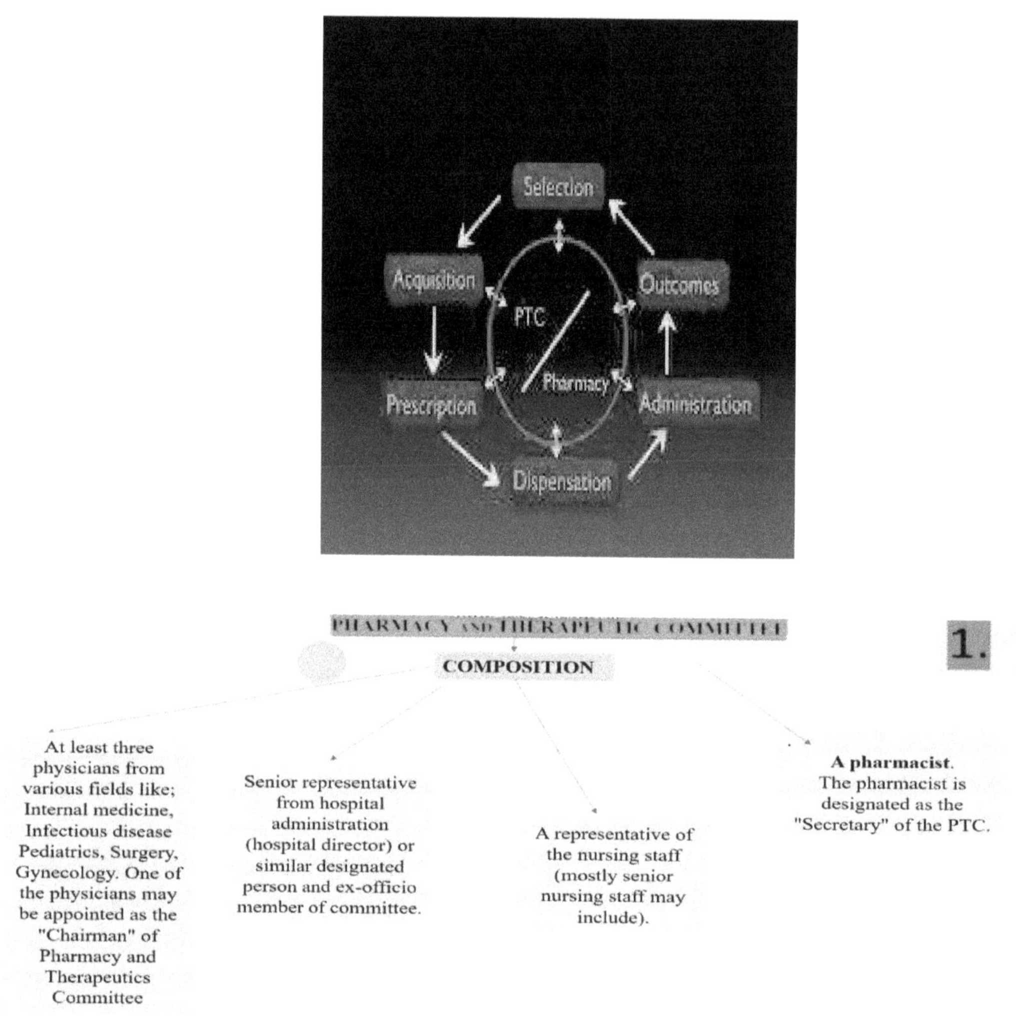

Operation of PTC:

This committee should meet regularly at least six times in the year and also as and when necessary. The committee can invite its meetings persons within or outside the hospital who can contribute specialized or unique knowledge, skills and judgements.

The agenda and the supplementary materials should be prepared by the Secretary and furnished to the committee members well in advance so that the members can study them properly before the meeting.

A typical agenda may consists of the following categories in general:

1) Minutes of the previous meeting.

2) Review of the contents of the Hospital Formulary for purpose of bringing it up to date, and deleting of products not considered necessary for use;

3) Information regarding new drugs which may have become commercially available.

4) Review of side effects, adverse drug reactions, toxic effects, drug interactions of drugs reported by various units of the hospital

5. And brought to notice of the committee by DIC.

6) Review of Drug Safety in the hospital.

7) Reports of various sub-committees.

8) Report of medical audit.

9) Any other matter with the permission of chair.

10) Vote of thanks. The minutes of all meeting hold should be prepared by the secretary and a permanent records of these minutes should maintained in the hospital.

Role of PTC in Drug-Safety

Drug safety includes responsibility from dispensing of drugs to drug-administration and then to observe possible adverse effects. PTC can play a major role in ensuring the drug-safety

Following guidelines may subserve the committee in asertaining the adequate safety factor of the hospital pharmacy.

1) A registered pharmacist – chief pharmacist -diploma holders

2) Not permit non-pharmacist perssonel

3) A sufficient numbers of qualified perssonel

 4) Adequate safe, work space, and storage facilities

5) Have equipment necessary

6) Automatic stop order-narcotics, hypnotics, anti coagulants

7) Firm policy-research drugs

8) Drug formulary

9) Out side its working hours

10) Poisonous materials- non poisionous materials

11) External use drugs-internal use drugs

12) Quality control measures, GMP during processing

13) Teaching programme

14) Periodical inspection

15) Adequate reference library

Role of PTC in Adverse Drug Monitoring: An ADR is defined as any unusual of unexpected harmful reaction including acute poisonings by narcotics, barbiturates, and amphetamines as well as industrial poisonings.

PROFORMA FOR MONITORING OF ADR IN INDIA

1. Do not leave any item blank

2. Mark tick in the appropriate box

3. Type or write in BLOCK LETTERS

19. 1)Centre Name: ---

 2)Type of patient: Inpatient(1) Outpatient(2)

3)Serial No:

4)Name of the patient:--------------------------------

5)Address(complete)--- --

--- Pin code--

6)Age:-----------------Years

7)Sex: Male(1) Female(2)

8)Occupation :--

9)Hospital Record No:

10)Registration Date:

11)Dietary Habit: Veg. (1) Non-Veg.(2)

12)Smoking habit: No (1) Yes(2) If yes, duration (yrs)

13)Alcoholic habit: No (1) Yes (2) If yes, duration (yrs)

14)Relevent Medical History: If yes, details ☐ Allergy No (1) Yes (2)--------------- ☐ Environmental exposure No (1) Yes (2)--------------- ☐ Occupational exposure No (1) Yes (2)---------------- ☐ Previous drug reaction No (1) Yes (2)--------------- ☐ Pregnancy 0/1/2/3 TRIMESTER------------------------ ☐ Family history of ADR No (1) Yes (2)---------------

15) Background signs / symptoms:--- --- --- ----- --

16) Provisional Diagnosis:

17) Treatment Schedule (including traditional medicines) ---
------------------------ Drug Indication Total Route Duration name daily Trade &(Diagnosis)
Generic dose --- ------------------------------
------------------------------- -- ----------------
----

18) Date of End of Treatment:

19) Outcome of Management: Recovered (1); Still under Rx (2); Died (3); Lost to follow up (4); ADR suspected

20) If ADR is suspected fill in the PROFORMA-II No (1) Yes (2)

Every case of adverse drug reaction must be first reported by the attending physician to the chairman of the PTC or clinical pharmacologist.

The attending physician should complete the 'Adverse Drug Reaction Report form' as illustrated above, on any patient having adverse reaction.

The medical record room will, upon the patients discharge, remove this report from the medical record and forward it to the chairman, who in turn periodically forward essential data to the central committee on Adverse Reactions formed by the State Government or the drug control authorities of the state, Government and the Drugs Controller or consultations with the bodies of experts such as Drugs Technical Advisory Board.

Automatic stop orders for Dangerous Drugs:

All Drug Orders for narcotics, sedatives, hypnotic anticoagulants, and antibiotics shall be automatically discontinued after 48 hours unless the order indicates an exact number of doses to be administered, or the attending physician, re-orders the medication.

All orders for narcotics, sedative and hypnotics must be rewritten every 24 hours.

In India, at present, this kind of system of issuing "ASODD" is not practiced except for hospitals like Christian Medical Hospital Vellore or Jaslok Hospital, Mumbai Escort group, Mayo Hospital etc.

Role of PTC in Developing "Emergency Drug Lists"

Since time factor is of very great urgency to most true emergency situations, it is absolutely necessary for the PTC of a hospital to get prepared boxes containing emergency drugs which should be always available readily for use at the bed-side.

List of such drugs and other supplies should be complied by the committee, and it should find their place in emergency kits

A) Supplies to be maintained in Emergency Box:

i. Syringes of various range Two each of 1 ml. i.e tuberculin or insulin syringe, 2 ml. syringe and 5 ml. syringe; and one each of 10ml and 20ml syringe.

ii. Needles, preferebly two each of 16', 18', 20', 21', 23', and 26',

iii. Files for breaking the ampoule

iv. Torniquets

v. Airway equipment

vi. Ryles tube

B) Drugs for Emergency Box:

These may selected in consultation with the physician but the following list is illustrative only i. Aminophylline 0.25 g/ml

ii. Amylnitrite glass capsules for inhalation

iii. Atropine sulphate 0.4mg/ml

iv. Caffeine sodium benzoate 0.5g/2 ml.

v. Calcium Gluconate 1 g/10 ml

vi. Digoxin 0.25 mg/ml

Diphenylhydantoin sodium 50 mg/ml

Epinephrine Hcl/1 mg/ml

☐ Heparin 10.000 units/ml

☐ Hydrocortisone 100mg

☐ Magnesium sulphate injection 10%, 50%

☐ Isoproterenol 1:100

☐ Mannitol injection 25%

☐ Nalorphine Hcl-10 mg/2ml

☐ Neostigmine methyl sulphate 0.25mg/ml

☐ Norepinephrine Injection 0.2%

☐ Pentobarbitone 50mg/ml

☐ Pentzocine

☐ Phenylephrine Hcl 10mg/ml

☐ Pheomethazone inj

☐ Picrotoxin Inj. 3mg/ml

☐ Procainamide 100mg/ml.

☐ Protmine sulphate 20mg/ml

☐ Saline for Injection 09% 30ml

☐ Sodium molar lactate solution

☐ Water for injection 20ml

C) Supplies for Cabinet Utility Room

i. Venuous cannulation set .

ii. Each set 12&17 venous catheters

iii. Pieces 6''shock blocks

iv. Oxygen catheters

v. Sterile suction catheters

vi. Razor with blades

vii. Package sterile gelatine sponge

viii. Resuscitation tube.

D) Other emergency supplies

i. Resuscitation carts

ii. Phlebotomy sets

iii. Oxygen equipments

iv. Tracheotomy sets

v. Dextran and tubing

vi. Burn sheets NB: Each hospital may modify this list by adding or deleting items as found necessary.

Role of PTC in Drug Product Defect Reporting Programme:

The drugs purchased by hospital may be defective in quality. It is for the committee to get information about the defective drug products and to inform it first to the manufacturer for appropriate action.

If satisfactory answer is not obtained from the manufacturer or supplier, it should be reported to the Food and Drug Control Administration.

Phone No.--------------

XYZ HOSPITAL Address -------------- Date received -------------

HOSPITAL PHARMACIST'S DRUG DEFECT REPORT

Reference No.-----------------------

1. Trade Name--------------Dosage form---------------- Strength-----------------------

2. Lot No.--------------------Expiry Date------------------

3. Date Purchased------------------

4. Name of the supplier---------------------------------------

5. Name and address of the manufacturer---

----- -----------

6. Reporting pharmacist's name----------------------------

7. Defects noted or suspected-- ----------------------

    Date---------   Signature of the chairman of PTC

Role of PTC in Drug Utilization Review:

Drug utilization includes prescribing, dispensing, administering and ingesting of prescription of drugs. Hospital pharmacist should take medication history that should include following information.

1) Medication being taken at the time of admission, during admission, home remedies (OTC) drugs.

2) Drug-allergies and idiosyncrosy towards food products etc.

XYZ HOSPITAL

PATIENT MEDICATION PROFILE   Record No----- Name

of the patient------------- Age------------ Sex---------

Address------------------------------------- DOA-----------

Admission Diagnosis--- Other Pathology------------------

Pre Operative Medications Used-------------------------------

Date	Drugs	Dose	Route	Started	Discontinued	Remarks

1. To help improved drug prescribing practices by promoting the safe and rational use of the drugs.

2. To detect and help prevent drug-interactions.

3. To help detect and prevent adverse drug reactions.

4. To detect and prevents IV additive incompatibilities.

5. To detect drug-induced diseases.

6. To detect possible drug-induced diseases.

7. To help detect and potential drug-toxicities.

PTC is the backbone of the hospital pharmacy and its services, and therefore, it should properly organized

DRUG INFORMATION SERVICES

It is a current, critically examined, relevant data about drugs and drug use in a given patient or situation" – Current information – Critically examined information – Relevant information.

Drug information means providing clinically relevant information on any aspect of drug. information provided is current, critically examined, relevant data about drugs and drug use in a given patient or situation.

DIC is an area where pharmacist specialised in providing information to health professionals or the public. ' A drug information centre (DIC) is a service unit operated by trained healthcare professionals, who are committed to providing drug information as it related to therapies, Pharmacoeconomics, education and research programs.

Request about drug information by medical students, interns, physicians, pharmacists and other health care professionals, patients or general public

The drug information request is recieved by the staff of the DIC preferably, pharmacologists, clinical pharmacologists and/or pharmacists

The various authentic sources of drug information (primary , secondary and/or tertiary) are referred to search for specific responses to the queries

The staff of the DIC responds to the query of the inquirer by telephone calls or written report. The DIC can also disseminate the drug information in the form of publications, guidelines or policy decisions

The requisitions received by the DICs are recorded in a standard form for future reference

HISTORY

First DIC was developed in university of Kentucky in 1962.

In united states 80% of the hospitals having DIC.

In Australia and the United Kingdom, the first drug information centres were established in 1968 at the royal Melbourne hospital, Victoria and in 1969 at the London hospital respectively. First drug information centre at Christian medical college, Vellore in the early 1970s.

DIC RESOURCES

Primary Literature	Secondary Literature	Tertiary Literature
• Original articles • (randomized controlled clinical trials, nonrandomized, prospective, clinical , trials, cohort studies, case-control studies, case series, and case reports)	• Medline • EMBASE • PubMed • Google Scholar • Iowa Drug Information System • (IDIS) • Journal watch • LexisNexis • BIOSIS • International Pharmaceutical • Abstracts (IPA) • Cochrane Library • Current Contents • CINAHL	• General textbooks • General product information (Drug Facts and Comparisons, Physicians' Desk Reference, Drug Information Handbook, Clinical Pharmacology, UpToDate, etc.) • Review articles • Treatment guidelines • Electronic textbooks and databases

PRIMARY SOURCE:

Information is presented by authors without any evaluation by a second party.

Provides must current information about drugs.

EXAMPLES: Articles published in journals (e.g. British medical journal), thesis etc…

SECONDARY SOURCE:

The original source has been evaluated by second party other than the publisher.

Modified and rearrange form

EXAMPLE; Review of primary reports, Medline, Lexicomp, Micromedex

TERTIARY SOURCE:

Information obtained from primary and secondary source and arranged in a manner to represent a composite of the available information.

EXAMPLE; Printed textbooks, reference book, formulary manuals. eg; oxford text book of medicine national formulary of India.

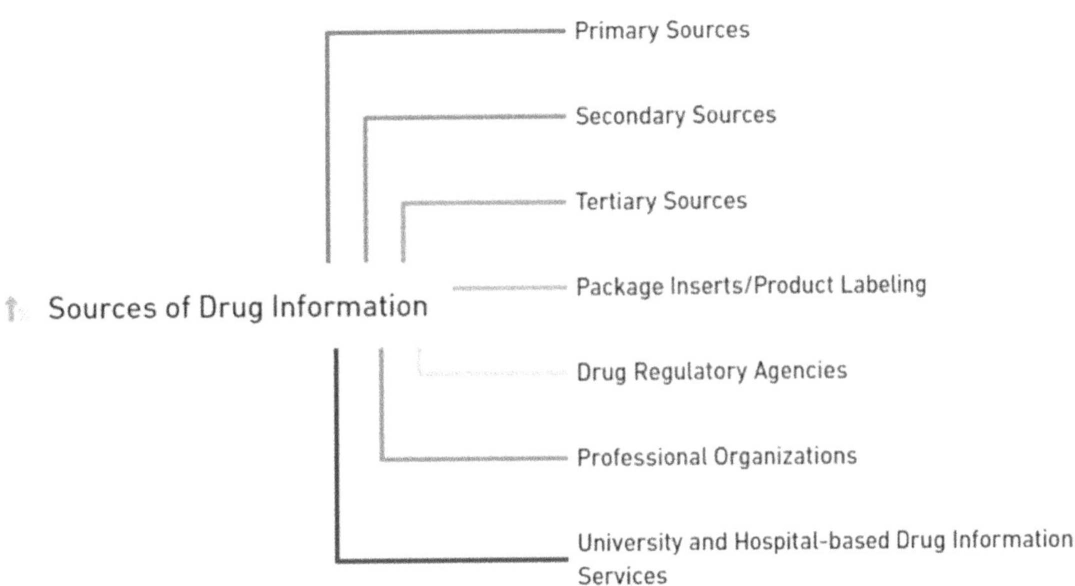

Need of Drug Information

The number of drugs in the international market has increased very much.

The newer drugs are generally more potent & selective, and formulation becoming increasingly complex.

The literature on drug has also expanded and covers a wide range of information.

To introduce a new drug into the practice, the professionals need to evaluate the given information.

A simple, quick reference to a pharmacopoeia or formulary is no longer sufficient.

AIMS AND OBJECTIVES OF DRUG INFORMATION CENTRE

To provision of information to health professionals on specific problems related to the use of drugs in particular patients.

The provision of information to officials in government agencies to optimize the decision-making process.

The preparation and development of guidelines and formularies.

To improve patient compliance and to provide a guide to responsible self-medication.

To develop and participate in continuing education programs.

To participate in undergraduate and graduate teaching programs.

To develop educational activities regarding the appropriate use of drugs for patient in the community

To prepare and distribute material on drugs to health personnel in the form of a drug information bulletin and/ or other media. ' To develop and participate in research programs.

ROLE OF CLINICAL PHARMACIST IN DIC

Communicates information about the services available.

Responds to queries accordingly to the degree of urgency.

Maintains a documented system for recording details of the query & enquirer.

Maintains documents for recording various responses to queries.

Records the queries & their response references.

Stores drug information service documents.

Ensures the service is evaluated at regular intervals.

Seek regular feedback from users that the drug information service has been provided in a timely and satisfactory manner.

Perform quality assurance of the information which has provided for improved quality of service.

clinical pharmacist who is contributed to establishing drug information service which is most useful for the prescribers and/or other professionals is termed as passive intervention.

To evaluate drug interventional service provided by clinical pharmacist in a tertiary care teaching hospital.

To provide drug information by direct approach and query boxes and finding the efficacy ratio by feedback process.

To identify and rectify DRP's with the suggestions of physicians.

To analyse its benefits in optimizing quality and safety of medication use.

To conduct the reactive and passive interventions ☐ To evaluate the quality of drug information service provided.

List Of Drug Information Centre in India

Andhra Pradesh state pharmacy council, Andhra Pradesh.

Bowring and lady Curzon hospital, Bangalore, Karnataka.

Christian medical college hospital, Vellore, Tamil Nadu.

Drug information centre, Victoria hospital, Bangalore.

Jawaharlal Nehru medical college hospital (JNMC), Belgaum, Karnataka

JSS, Ooty, Tamil Nadu

JSS, Mysore, Karnataka.

DIC IN ABROAD

The university of RHODE ISLAND.

University of southern Queensland, Australia

Griffith University, Australia

University of Wyoming, USA

University of Findley, USA

PATIENT COUNSELLING

Patient counselling is defined as providing medication information, advice and assistance to help the patient use their medication appropriately.

It can be provided orally or in written form to the patients or their representatives.

May include information on directions of use, advice on side effects, precautions, storage, diet and life style modifications.

AIM / OBJECTIVES

Improve patient understanding of their illness & role of medicine

Improve medication adherence

Reduce incidence of medication errors, ADR, unnecessary healthcare costs

Prevent drug interactions

Improve QOL

Improve professional rapport between patient & pharmacist.

Communication skills for effective counselling

Verbal Skills: Language Tone Speed Volume

Non-Verbal Skills: Proximity Facial Expression Body language Eye contact

Proximity:

It refers to the distance that people maintain themselves during the counseling process. Classified into:

1. Intimate: 45cm or less

2. Personal: 45cm to 1.2m

3. Social: 1.2-3.6m

4. Public > 3.6 m

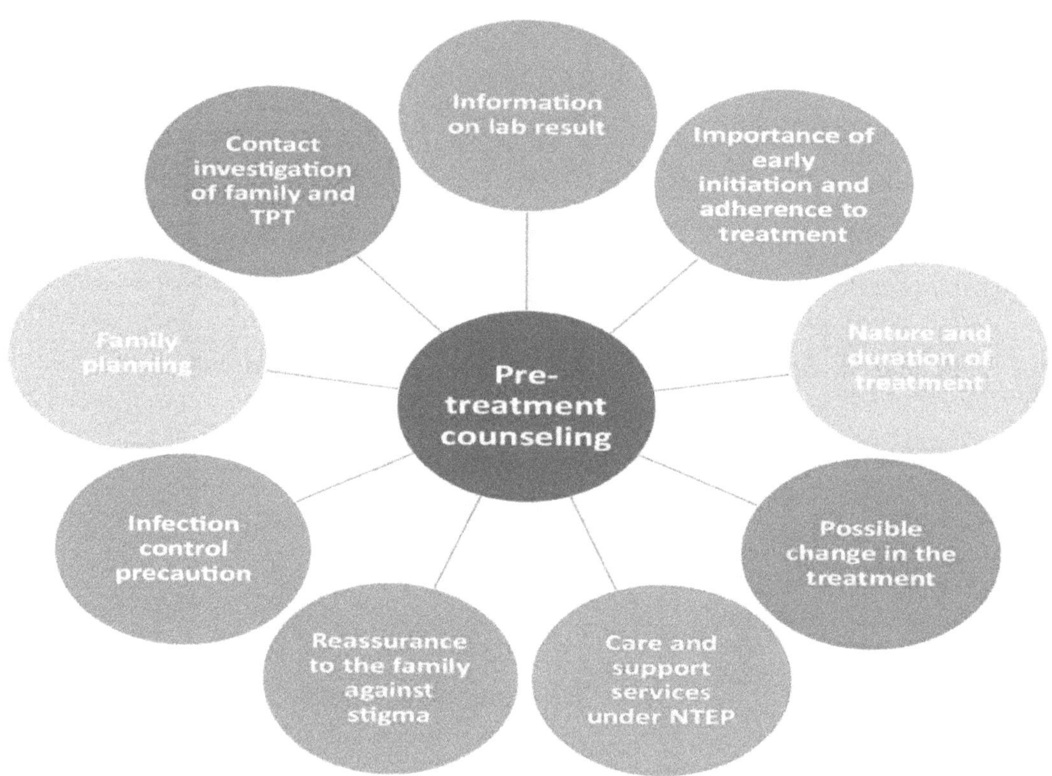

QUALITIES OF A GOOD COUNSELOR

Be a good listener

Be flexible

Be empathetic

Be non- judgmental

Be tolerant

Communicate confidently Pharmacist has to give unbiased and authentic information in a most professional manner

Steps of Patient Counselling

Preparing for the counselling

Opening the counselling

Counselling Content

Closing the Lecture

Preparing for the Lecture

Success of counselling depends on knowledge & skill of the counsellor Know about the patient & his/ her treatment details

Hospital setting- refer patient case notes

Community setting- prescription, a record of previous dispensing

Know mental and physical state of the patient

Opening the Lecture

Introduce your self

Explain purpose of counselling

Obtain drug related information such as allergies, use of alternative medicine etc.

Assess the patients understanding of the disease and treatment

Eg: What did the doctor tell you about your illness?

What do you know about your disease? Can u tell me the symptoms you have been experiencing?

Use open ended questions

Counselling Content

Heart of the counselling Lecture

Pharmacist explains the patient

About the disease

About the medication

About lifestyle modifications

Counselling Content

Name & strength of the medication

Reason why it has been prescribed

How it works

Directions for administering the medicine

        – How often to take the medicine

        – How much to take at one time

        – How long it will be necessary to take the medicine

        – When to take it : before, during, after meals? At bed time? At any other special times?

        – How to take it? With water? With fruit juice? How much?

        – What to do if you forget to take it (miss a dose)

        -Foods, drinks, or other medicines that you should not take while taking the medicines

        – Restrictions on activities while taking the medicine

        – Possible side effects. What to do if they appear. How to minimize the side effects. How soon they will go away.

        – When to seek help if they are problems

        – How long to wait before reporting no change in symptoms.

        – How to store the medicine

        – The expiration date

– The cost of the medicine

– How to have your prescription refilled, if necessary

– Necessity to complete the course.

– Drug-Drug, Drug-Food interactions

Closing the Lecture

Before closing the Lecture, it is essential to check patients understanding

Ask feedback questions

Eg: 1. Can you remember what this medication is for?

2. For how long you should take this medication?

3. Ask whether patient has any doubts / questions?

Encourage patient to contact pharmacist if they need further advice/ information

Closing the Lecture

1. Verify the patient's understanding by means of feedback

2. Summarize by emphasizing key points

3. Give an opportunity to the patient to put forward any concerns.

4. Help the patient to plan follow-up

Counselling Aids

Medication cards: written summary of patient's medication which is easy to understand Patient information leaflets

Visual aids Leaflets on how to use ear drops, eye ointments, pessaries, suppositories, nebulizer etc.

COMMON MEDICATIONS FLASHCARDS

300 CARDS — **38 TOPICS** — **100+ VISUALS** — **250+ STICKERS** — **DIGITAL + PRINTABLE**

H2 Receptor Antagonists

Definition

H2 receptor antagonists (H2RAs), also known as H2 blockers, are a class of medications that reduce stomach acid production by blocking histamine receptors on the parietal cells of the stomach.

Common

Extrapyramidal Symptoms (EPS) and Neuroleptic Malignant Syndrome (NMS)

Risk and Management

- Akathisia: Beta-blockers (e.g. anticholinergics
- Parkinsonism: Anticholinergic
- Tardive Dyskinesia: Gradual different antipsychotic with a medications like valbenazine

Nursing Considerations

- Assessment: Regularly monitor for signs of EPS and educate patients on reporting symptoms early.
- Patient Education: Educate patients about the potential for EPS and the importance of early reporting and management.

blood pressure, blood

siderations

baseline and regularly during treatment.
- Patient Education: Educate patients on the importance of a healthy lifestyle and regular monitoring to prevent and manage metabolic syndrome.

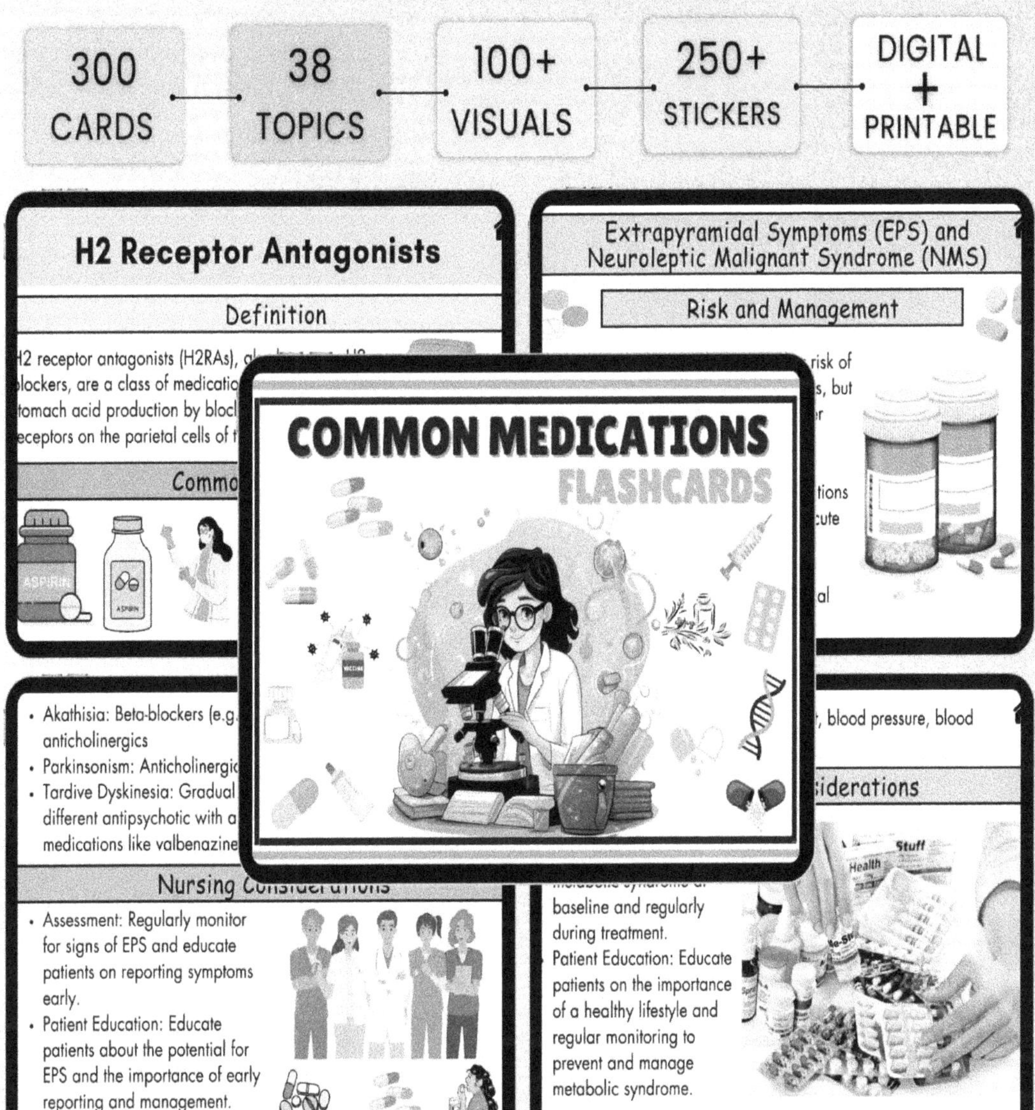

Type 2 Diabetes Mellitus

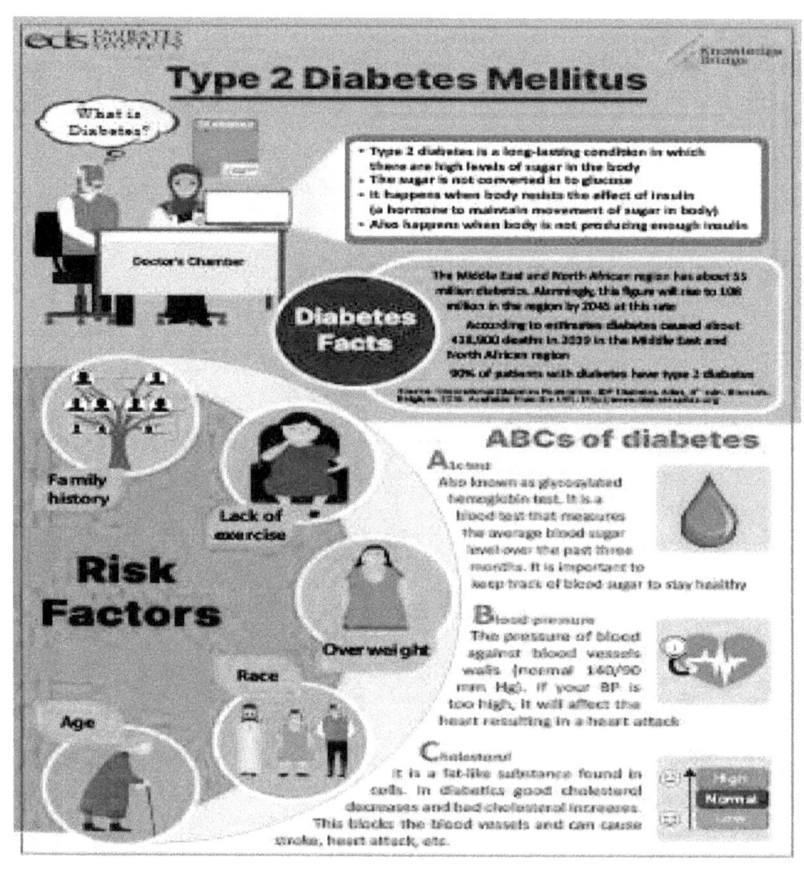

EDUCATION AND TRAINING PROGRAM IN THE HOSPITAL

It is scientific process of improving the knowledge and skills of employee for doing a particular job.

The main purpose of training is to mould the behaviour of new recruits so that they can do their job in a more efficient way.

In hospitals education and training activity includes undergraduate and graduate programme in medicine, teaching student nurses, training of technologist, physiotherapist, dietician, administrative residents, social service worker and pharmacist.

Role of Pharmacist

Educating the medical and allied health professional as well as the patients

Participate in education program related to different medical area such as psychiatric, physical, rehabilitation, special education program like diabetic or cardiac patient

Involve in education of student nurses, training of graduate nurses, undergraduate as well as graduate pharmacy student or students in hospital pharmacy programmes

Involve in internal and external teaching activity

Educate general public through lecture or demonstration about the rational use of drugs and their dosages

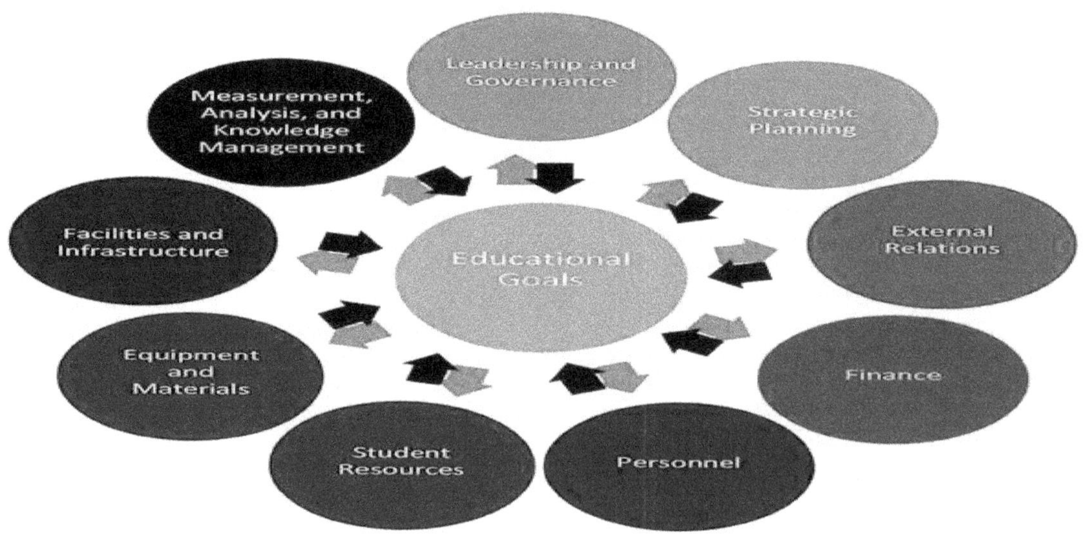

Internal Teaching Programme

Training of students nurses

Seminar for graduate nurses, house staff and medical staff

Training undergraduate students in hospital pharmacy

Patient teaching programme

Training clinical pharmacist

Training residents in hospital administration

External Teaching Programme

Any teaching activity performed by pharmacist outside the hospital

Participation in seminar, refresher course

Participation in activities of nursing, dietary, oxygen therapy and medical technology

Preparation of manuscript for publication in professional press

Obtain various grant-in-aid to support research in drug distribution techniques or prescription techniques

Participate in educational activities organized during annual session of professional bodies such as Indian Pharmaceutical congress

Code of Ethics for Community Pharmacy: The code defines and seeks to clarify the obligations of pharmacist to use their own knowledge and skills for the benefit of others, to minimize harm, to respect patient autonomy and to provide fair and just pharmacy care for their patients

For those entering the profession, the code identifies the basic moral commitments of pharmacy care and serves as a source for education and reflection

Professional ethics are defined as rules of "conduct or standards by which a professional community regulates its actions and sets standards for its members"

Code of Ethics Principle

Principles 1 –Pharmacists respect the professional relationship with the patient and acts with honesty, integrity and compassion.

Principle 2. Pharmacists honour the individual needs, values and dignity of the patient

Principle 3- Pharmacists support the right of the patient to make personal choices about pharmacy care

Principle 4- Pharmacist provide a complete care to the patients and actively supports the patients right to receive competent and ethical care

Principle 5- Pharmacists protects the patients right of confidentiality

Principle 6- Pharmacists respect the values and abilities of the colleagues and other health professionals

Principle 7- Pharmacists Endeavour to ensure that the practice environment contributes to safe and effective pharmacy care

Principle 8- Pharmacists ensure continuity of care in the event of job action, pharmacy closure or conflict with moral benefits

Advantages of code of ethics

The code provides clear direction for avoiding ethical violations

The code tries to provide guidance for those pharmacists who face ethical problems

Role of pharmacist in interdepartmental communication

Departmental administration

Interdepartmental activity

Inpatient drug distribution and control

Ambulatory patient services

Clinical services

Drug information services

Education and training

Technology and quality control activity

Education And Training Program in Hospital:

Proper implementation of education and training programs on safe patient handling to all hospital staff

Demonstration on the use of the equipment and its maintenance in the safe handling of patients

Ideas of education and training for safe patient handling:

All appropriate workers should be trained on using mechanical equipment.

Involve patients and their families.

Care givers should be trained to check each patient's mobility every time.

Consider supporters and peer education champions.

In the hospital, there may operate several practices under training and development program amongst these, following are the seven best practices:

1. Generate training programs that have different learning styles

2. Organization of interactive programs 3. Introduce the computer-based training modules.

4. Display the specific information/practices in the hospital.

5. Ensure the training reproduces changing skills. 6. Consider employee demands beyond training.

7. Evaluate the effectiveness of training programs.

Training Programs in Hospital

To perform their task better, improve their work- related skill set, increase knowledge about their work, become aware of their future roles and responsibilities related to their task

Training is the process of instructing required knowledge, skills, and attitudes to the employees to enhance their existing skills, knowledge, and attitudes, and progresses into newer ones.

Hospital authority plays an important role in designing, organizing, and delivery of required training courses for the employees

PRESCRIBED MEDICATION ORDER AND COMMUNICATION SKILLS

Prescribed medication order is the written directions which are the primary means by which prescribers communicate with pharmacists regarding the specific treatment regimen for a patient.

The prescribers may also give medication orders verbally or non-verbally to a registered/licensed pharmacist or nurse.

While the medications are sold only on clear, complete, and signed prescription orders.

Medication orders are needed to must have the following points:

Patient name.

Name of medication.

Strength of medication.

Dose.

Dosage form.

Time or frequency of administration.

Route of administration.

Quantity to dispense.

Prescriber name and signature.

Refill authorization.

Date.

PRN medication orders should specify the frequency of administration, maximum daily dosage, and condition for which the medication is being administered.

Interpretation of Prescriptions

Drug use is a complex process and there are many drugs related challenges at various levels involving prescribers, pharmacists, and patients.

While medications misadventure can occur anywhere in the health care system from prescribers to the dispenser to administration and finally to patient use.

While many errors can be preventable and pharmacists play important role in the appropriate dispensing of prescribed medications.

By interpreting the proper abbreviation involved in the prescription one can effectively interpret the prescription and avoid errors.

The following table mentioned the interpretation of commonly used abbreviations and Latin terms while prescribing.

LATIN TERMS AND ABBREVIATIONS USED IN PRESCRIPTION		
ABBREVIATIONS	**LATIN TERM/PHRASE**	**ENGLISH MEANING**
1. a., applic.	applicantus. a, um	to be applied
2. aa	ana	of each
3. a.c., ant.cib.	ante cibum	before food
4. ad	ad	to sufficient or to produce
5. addend	addendus. a, um	to be added
	addendo	by adding
6. a.h., alt. hor.	alternis horis	every other hour
7. a.j.	ante jentaculum	before breakfast
8. alt. die	alterno die	every other day
9. aq. calid.	aqua calida	hot water
10. aq. dest.	aqua destillata	distilled water
11. aq. frig.	aqua frigida	cold water
12. aug.	augeatur	let it be increased
13. aur.	auris	the ear
14. b.	bis	twice
15. b.d., b.i.d.	bis die, bis in die	twice daily
16. b.t.d., b.t.i.d.	bis terve in die	two or three times a day
17. c.c	cum cibos	with food
18. c.l.q.s.	cuilibet quantum sufficiat	a sufficient quality or as you please
19. cap.	cape	take
	capitat	let him take
	capiatur	let it be taken
	capiantur	let them be taken
	capiendus, a, um	to be taken
20. comp.	composites, a, um	compound
21. coch.	cochleare	spoonful
22. conc.	concentrates, a, um	concentrate
23. d.d.	de die	daily
24. d, in p. aeq.	divide in partes aequales	divide into equal parts
25. d.p.	directione propria	with proper directions
26. decub. hor.	decubitas hora	at bedtime
27. dext.	dexter	right, on the right
28. dil.	dilutes, a, um	diluted
29. div.	divide	divide
30. dol. urg.	dolore urgente	when the pain is severe
31. dolent. part.	dolente parti	to the afflicted part
32. dup., dx.	duplex	double
33. dur.	durus	hard
34. dur. dol	durante dolore	when the pain lasts
35. e.m.p.	ex modo praescripto	in the manner prescribed
36. e. paul. aq.	ex paulo aquae	in a little water
37. ex	ex	from out of
38. ex aq.	ex aqua	with water
39. ex. aq. coch. ampl.	ex aqua cochleari amplo	in a tablespoonful of water
40. extempl.	extemplo	immediately
41. f., fft.	fiat	let it be made
	fiant	let them be made

Legal Requirements

A PRN protocol is required for PRN medication orders which are ordered on a daily/regular basis. So, such medication orders should specify the frequency of administration, maximum daily dosage, and the condition for which medication is being administered.

The PRN protocol provides additional information regarding the medication order and to understand the pharmacist when and how much of the prescribed medication to give.

The PRN protocol should include the following points: All of the information is found in the regular medication order, along with the –

The specific signs and symptoms for which the medication should be given to a patient.

A maximum daily dosage.

Any special instructions, for example, when to call prescribing practitioner or nurse.

Communication Skills

Communication skills are the capability to use language in precise and express information in an easy way to understand with patients and family members, other physicians, nurses, pharmacists, and other health care providers.

Effective communication skills are a critical element for patients, pharmacists, and doctors.

Following are the three main goals of communication:

1. Creating good interpersonal relationships.
2. Facilitating the exchange of information.
3. Including patients in decision making.

Poor communication skills between pharmacist and patient may lead to the following:

1. Inaccurate patient medication history.
2. Inappropriate therapeutic decisions
3. Leads to patient confusion, patient disinterest, and patient non-compliance.

Communicating with Health Professionals: Effective communication between pharmacist and physicians, nurses, and other pharmacists are essential. Following are some instructions and advantages of effective and clear communications between different health professionals involved in patient care services:

1. Good doctor-patient communication has the potential to help in regulating patient's emotions, facilitate comprehension of medical information, and allow for better identification of patient's needs perceptions, and expectations.

2. Patient's report good communication is more likely to be satisfied with their health care, and especially relevant information for accurate diagnosis of their problems, follow the advice and adhere to the prescribed treatment.

3. A more patient-centred communication may provide satisfactory results from the patient as well as from the doctor.

4. A pharmacist must notify within a reasonable time after renewing the prescription.

5. Pharmacists are periodically required to contact prescribers to manage drug interaction or suggest changes to therapy that could ensure the best possible patient outcomes.

6. Manage the drug-related problem by providing your therapeutic recommendation to the prescriber including how to manage this situation.

7. Always endeavour to include a reference to the evidence that supports your recommendations this can increase the prescribers comfort level with this and future recommendations.

8. Effective written communication to prescribers is essential to provide appropriate and comprehensive patient care.

9. Reducing the risks associated with unclear messaging promotes patient safety and quality care.

Communication between Prescribers and Patients: Effective patient counselling can assist patients in using their medicines safely and reliably. Before giving information, check the patient's level of understanding. Advice the patient to adapt the medication regimen to their life style. Following are some types of communication required for collecting the information and instructing with patients by health practitioners.

1. **Medication History Interviews are required for making decisions.**

The following information is recorded while communicating with patients:

> Currently or recently prescribed medicines.
>
> OTC medicines purchased.
>
> Vaccinations.
>
> Alternative or traditional remedies.
>
> Description of reactions and allergies to medicines.
>
> Medicines were found to be ineffective.

2. **Patient Information Leaflet (PILs):**

> Practitioners should use the following outline key information to help/assist the patients and their caregivers/family members in the effective, clear, and safe uses of medicines. The following information should be included while prescribing the medication as well as to be instructed verbally in easy language which can understand the patient, their family members as well as pharmacist and nurses , Trade and a generic name.
>
> Indications for which the medicines are being taken.
>
> Dosage administrative advice and instructions.
>
> Information on the action required if a dose is missed.

Common or serious side effects may occur due to drug administration.

Storage condition for prescribed medications information.

Action to be taken if a side effect is an experience.

Name and contact details of the hospital/physician or health care provider should be provided.

Author and date of publication of the information.

BUDGET PREPARATION AND IMPLEMENTATION

Definition: Budget is defined as a financial or quantitative statement prepared for given the purpose of attaining the objective.

It is an instrument through which hospital administration, management at departmental levels, and the governing board can review the hospital's services in relationship to a prepared plan in a comprehensive and integrated form expressed in financial terms.

Objectives of budget

- Development of standards
- Comparison of actual results with standards
- Identification of deviation or fluctuation
- Analysis of deviation effectively manage the financial aspects of the responsible person will use the budget
- Details to determine whether the proposal is economically feasible and realistic.
- To monitor the hospital financial activities
- Estimate the cost of completing objectives identified in the proposal.

Types of budget preparation:

Based on the duration of budget, it can be divided in to:

> Short term budget (2 years)
>
> Long term budget (5 - 10 years)

Based on the organizational structure of hospital budget, it can be divided in to:

> Centralized budget
>
> Decentralized budget

Centralized Budget Preparation

The centralization of pharmacy drug budgets is supported by the 1993 medication safety guidelines of the American Society of Hospital Pharmacists (now the American Society of Health System Pharmacists), which recommended that "the pharmacy department must be responsible for the procurement, distribution, and control of all drugs used within the organization".

The Pharmacist, in order to participate more effectively in the budgetary process, must be familiar with the certain aspects of the process such as:

> 1. Personal considerations
>
> 2. Development of confidence among other officials
>
> 3. Institutional policies
>
> 4. Demographical pressures

1. Personal considerations:

Personal considerations such previous experience in the furnishing of budget with thorough support justification has a better chance of approval

2. Development of confidence among other officials:

As most of pharmacy activities affect the other departments of a hospital it is important for the chief pharmacist to secure their collaborations and support.

3. Institutional policies:

The Institutional policy considerations in the budgeting process consists of the aims and objectives of the hospital and its developments.

4. Demographical pressures:

Patient's representatives with a knowledge of demographic epidemiological and attitudes are part of several boards of trustees and hence in these circumstances pharmacist are able to provide the type services needed by the people.

Decentralized Budget Preparation

- The responsibility for drug budgets lies with each individual department and not solely with the pharmacy department.
- This approach can lead to an improvement in evidence-based practice, better patient outcomes, lower overall costs, and less wastage of medications, all without compromising the high quality of service that institutional pharmacies provide.
- If drug budgets are allocated to individual departments, hospital pharmacy departments will continue to play a vital role in various drug-related services, including procurement, storage, dispensing, and clinical and support services.
- With a decentralized system, it is still feasible to have a single formulary and a unified pharmacy and therapeutics committee.
- Pharmacists can still be involved in the development and maintenance of a cost effective, evidence-based formulary.

Centralized Vs Decentralized Budget Preparation

- Giving departments the authority to manage their own drug budgets tends to increase physicians' awareness of evidence-based practice
- The physicians were made aware of the economic implications of their choices
- In addition to increasing compliance with evidence-based practice, decentralization of drug budgets allows for overall cost savings

• Decentralization of the drug budget to individual departments and education of primary caregivers would empower physicians to become more responsible stewards of drug use

• Reducing drug wastage through education of prescribers is another potential benefit of decentralized drug budgets

• Increased awareness of costs may motivate providers to decrease their drug budgets, which can in turn lead to less drug wastage.

• Incorporating drugs into an individual departmental budget promotes prescription stewardship by physicians, removing the perception of pharmacists as the "drug budget police".

• Enforcement of prescribing according to a formulary would instead be the responsibility of each department head.

• Eliminating this "policing" role might allow for better interdisciplinary relation

• Decentralization of drug budgets increases overall costs by fostering fragmentation and inefficiencies within the hospital's medication management process

• The process of developing a drug budget is complex and time- intensive.

• In decentralized systems, each department must perform this process separately, whereas the process is more efficient and comprehensive in a centralized system

• Decisions related to drug budgets are associated with economic demands for the time of pharmacy personnel, including time required for retrieving and delivering medications, compounding IV admixtures, and managing drug packaging materials and technology.

• Decentralized decision-making results in an uneven distribution of goods and services to different wards, a decrease in standardization and efficiency, and increases in the cost-of-service provision

• In a decentralized system, stock must be segregated into several caches according to who "owns" the medications; this can lead to logistic challenges in storage and tracking.

• Assigning drug costs to each department as patients are transferred from one service to another is time-consuming and requires an information system to track and provide timely statistics on usage, costs, and supplies

• In contrast, a centralized system allows for procurement and stock- control processes that minimize acquisition costs and wastage. • These processes include monitoring of expiry dates, recycling of dispensed but unused medication, and strategic allocation of high- demand, back-ordered, or expensive drugs to areas of urgent need • In a decentralized system, each department has different formulary drug preferences and will argue for larger budgets based on its own baseline drug costs.

- In a centralized system, the pharmacy can effectively influence such costs by developing policies for therapeutic substitutions, automatic stop orders, and restricted drug use, tailoring them to departmental resources and hospital needs

  - Decentralized processes also compromise institutions' leverage on bulk buying contracts; in contrast, centralized tendering in a competitive bidding process yields the best price for the organization. • Increased drug stock in a decentralized system augments the risk of medication errors through the availability of multiple strengths or types of medications • Decentralization may precipitate conflicts of interest

Divisions of Budget

1. Income accounts or revenue accounts

2. Expenditure accounts

3. Capital Equipment and construction

Income accounts or revenue accounts

• Total income must be calculated for the implementation of the budget.

• A common method is, either the department of pharmacy or the accounting departments maintains a daily, weekly, monthly or annual total of the cost of the pharmaceuticals issued to the various patient services as well as to the special service department.

• These above incomes obtained from the processing of patient prescription and requisitions, represents the true income of the department.

• Other statistics that are of value in assisting management to accurately predict the volume of activity of the department of pharmacy are:

  1. Number of prescriptions according to subcategories.

  2. Number of prescriptions dispensed per pharmacist.

  3. Hours of service.

  4. Prescription volume per hour of service.

  5. Medication cost per patient day.

  6. Medication cost per clinic visit.

  7. Average drug cost per prescription.

• Generally, income in hospital pharmacy is limited to the sale of drugs to inpatients, ambulatory patients and departments of the hospital.

• The sale of drugs to patients may be subdivided further based upon patient's ability to pay or to their employment status if they are employed by the hospital.

  a) Full payment

b) Part payment

c) Non - payers

d) Physician (not paying)

e) General employee

Expenditure accounts:

Expense account in general may be divided into following:

1. Administrative and general expenses.

2. Professional care of the patients.

3. Out-patients and emergency expenses.

4. Miscellaneous expenses.

The expenditure accounts also include the following categories

1. Salaries and wages

2. Expenses of supplies & materials

3. Drugs and pharmaceutical expenses

4. Purchase expense

5. Miscellaneous supplies and expenses.

1. Salaries and Wages:

Includes salaries and wages of

(i)   Pharmacists,

(ii)   Assistants,

(iii)   Clerks and

(iv)   Others

It is important that the pharmacist gives break up of all salaries and wages paid.

The chief pharmacist subdivides the posts into further three categories viz. administrative, professional and non-professional staff.

The charts separate the full time and part time staff in above mentioned categories.

The costs of new posts are added and lastly any overtime, which according to past experience may be necessary.

The total of all these items constitutes the total anticipated salary and wage expenditure for the next financial year.

Inflows	₹	Outflows	₹
Opening balance:		Payment to creditors	90,000
Cash	10,000	Salaries and wages	25,000
Bank	70,000	Payment of overheads	15,000
Share capital - shares issued	5,00,000	Fixed assets acquired	4,00,000
Collection from Debtors	3,50,000	Debentures redeemed	50,000
Sale of fixed assets	70,000	Bank loan repaid	2,50,000
		Taxation	55,000
		Dividends	1,00,000
		Closing balance:	
		Cash	5,000
		bank	10,000
	10,00,000		10,00,000

Expenses Of Supplies & Materials:

1. Chief pharmacist or the responsible person should prepare the financial statement regarding the requirement of amount in rupees for supplies and materials with the help of the latest financial budget.

2. Necessary to show the actual cost of the materials.

3. If the budgeted figure and the previous figure was the same then the previously prepared budget was well prepared.

3. Drug and Pharmaceuticals:

• Those dispensed by prescriptions or otherwise from the hospital pharmacy department.

• Those used in the outpatient and emergency and other departments.

4. Purchase expense:

• This account should include the cost of prescription (excluding those intended for outpatient) purchased from outside pharmacy in case the hospital does not have its own Pharmacy.

5. Miscellaneous Supply and Expenses:

• Bottles, labels, glass wares, narcotics and alcoholic permit fees, printed forms and stationery, pharmacist uniforms, reference books etc.

• Parts required to rcpair and maintain equipment used by this department and repairs made by outside concerns also should be charged to this account.

• All the things mentioned will provide a guideline for the preparation and is changed according to the need of the hospital

Capital Equipment and construction

• In hospitals where funding of the depreciation of physical plant and equipment is practiced, the actual cash for replacement or remodeling is usually readily available.

• In those hospital where funding is not a policy, then construction and purchase of equipment creates a major financial burden requiring the development of a comprehensive and detailed budget.

• However, irrespective of the policy with regard to funding, an equipment and construction budget must be prepared.

List of Life period in years of depreciable machinery and equipment

Professional Equipment		Administrative Equipment
Balances	Prescription case	Bookcases
Cabinets (Metal or Wood)	Pressure Pumps, Vacuum Pumps	Bulletin Boards
Capsule machine	Refrigerator	Calculators, computers
Chemical hoods	Sterilizers	Clocks
Distilling apparatus	Tanks	Lockers, metal safes
Metallic filters	computers	worktables
Homogenizers	Tablet manufacturing Equipment	Filing, cabinets
Autoclaves	pH meter, Polari meter	Ledgers and accounts books

Implementation of budget:

It includes the following parameters

       1. Requirement of different departments

       2. Actual fund position

       3. Utility of particular item

       4. Cost of products

       5. Quantity of products

Advantages of planned the budget:

       1. Develop better financial planning.

       2. Gives a better focus on decision making to the management.

       3. Effectively manage the financial aspects of the hospital.

       4. Exposes the reasons of over expenditure.

       5. Helps to focus on hospital priorities

       6. Enhance efficiency of staffs and others.

Factors affecting budget:

1. Local conditions and compulsion

2. Management policy

3. Confidence of higher authorities

4. In ability of higher authorities

5. Unforeseen fluctuations in supply and demand

CLINICAL PHARMACY

Clinical pharmacy has come of age and the clinical pharmacist is now able to dispense knowledge as a product to patients and physicians.

• As new drugs were released on the market, pharmacy profession began to move towards, pharmacology, clinical therapeutics and pharmacokinetics.

• Hospital pharmacy seemed to take the lead in this clinical movement as several studies indicated that with many powerful drugs used in hospitals adverse reactions were a serious problem that needed the involvement of clinical services.

Objectives

• To assist the physicians in doing a better job of prescribing and monitoring drug therapy.

• To assists nurses in administering medications and documenting medication incidents correctly.

• To maximize the patients in the drug use process.

Scope of Clinical Pharmacy

1. **Obtain and prepare medication history of the patients on admission**

   It records past and present use of prescription and non-prescriptions drugs, drug allergies, adverse drug reactions associated with the medication and an estimate the patient's compliance with medication regimens.

2. **Monitoring Of Drug Therapy**

   This may be by direct involvement with the patient and routine evaluation of the patient's drug regimen medical problems, laboratory data and special procedures and communicating relevant findings and recommendations to other clinicians

3. **Patient Education and Counselling**

   • It involves providing information to the patients about their drug therapy.

   • To act as a source of information about health promotion and disease prevent amongst the public.

4. **Preparation in Medical Emergencies**

   • Keep important information handy

   • Have a hospital overnight bag packed

   • Educate yourself about emergency response

   • Discuss medical alert systems with your loved one

   • Plan to alternate care giving responsibilities

5.MANAGEMENT OF PATIENTS WITH CHRONIC DISEASE

• Eating healthy helps prevent, delay, and manage heart disease, type 2 diabetes, and other chronic diseases

• Get Screened

• Get Regular Physical Activity

• Get Enough Sleep

• Avoid Drinking Too Much Alcohol

6. Participation in Clinical Drug Investigation

• Pharmacist collaborates with physician investigators for conducting clinical drug trials.

7.Participation In Education of Medical Professionals and Nursing Personnels in Patient Care Areas

•These education programs for nurses and physicians include formal and informal education pertaining to the safe and effective use of drug therapy.

Status Of Clinical Pharmacy in India

• Hospital pharmacy in India has not made success beyond purchase, storage, dispensing and distribution of drugs.

• In some hospitals, especially in big hospitals, it has started manufacturing of infusion fluid and eye drops.

• Excellent relationship with the medical profession is needed to ensure progress of clinical pharmacy.

• Rewarding career path with opportunities to contribute to improved medication use

• Employment in hospitals, teaching, drug information, pharmacovigilance, clinical research, medical information.

Barriers in the development of clinical pharmacy

• Lack of pharmacist's attitudes

• Lack of advanced practice skills

• Lack of resource-related constraints

• Lack of system-related constraints

• Lack of academic/educational obstacles

• Lack of interprofessional obstacles

• Lack knowledge

• Lack of Team approach

• Lack of Motivation

PEDIATRICS: • Paediatrics is the specialty of medical science concerned with the physical, mental, and social health of children from birth to young adulthood. Paediatric care encompasses a broad spectrum of health services ranging from preventive health care to the diagnosis and treatment of acute and chronic diseases.

• The newborn maturity rating scale is assessed by New Ballard scale

• Normal pulse rate in infants 110-160 beat/min.

•Significance of pediatrics

• Major consumers of health care.

• 35-40% of total population are children below the age of 15.

• More vulnerable to various health problems.

• Majority of Childs morbidity & mortality preventable.

• Needs special care to survive & thrive. Some common medicines for paediatrics √ Amoxicillin √ Fluticasone √Amoxicillin/Clavulanic Acid √ Ibuprofen √ Nystatin √ Albuterol √ Cefdinir √ Cephalexin √ Montelukast Sodium/Singulair √ Azithromycin √ Rednisone

GERIATRICS:

• A branch of medicine that deals with the problems and diseases of old age and the medical care and treatment of aging people.

• Geriatrics, or geriatric medicine, is a medical specialty focused on providing care for unique health needs of older adults.

• Age related physiological change in geriatric patient which may affect drug distribution is by increased total body water. Significance of Geriatrics

• Patient education & motivation

• Oral examination

• Nutrition counselling

• Teaching of tooth brushing & flossing methods

• Teaching of maintaining natural teeth (if exist)

• Teaching of care for false teeth, Checking of artificial dentures for proper fitting Some common medicines for Geriatrics √ Amlodipine besylate √ Azithromycin √ Levothyroxine √ Lisinopril √ Metformin √ Omeprazole √ Simvastatin

ANTI-NATAL CARE

Routine antenatal care (ANC) is defined as the care provided by health practitioners (or others) to all pregnant women to ensure the best health conditions for the women and their foetuses during pregnancy. Significance of anti-natal care

• To ensure that the pregnant woman and her foetus are in the best possible health.

• To detect early and treat properly complications Offering education for parenthood

• To prepare the woman for labor, lactation and care of her infant.

POST -NATAL CARE:

World health organization stated that postnatal care is defined as a care given to the mother and her newborn baby immediately after the birth of the placenta and for the first six weeks of life. The care of provided to women and their Newborns for the first few months following Childbirth Significance of post-natal care

• To prevent maternal & neo natal tetanus.

• To facilitate health education regarding diet, rest, avoidance of unnecessary travel & preparation for delivery

Daily activities of clinical pharmacist: Definition, goal and procedure of

•Ward round participation

•Treatment chart review

•Adverse drug reaction monitoring

•Drug information and poisons information • • •

Daily Activities of Clinical Pharmacists

1.WARD ROUND PARTICIPATION

•Various countries have shown pharmacist participation in ward round helps patient as well as other health care professionals.

• Addition of pharmacist participation in ward rounds helps ensure safe effective and economic use of drugs which ultimately results in decreased adverse drug events improved patients care, reduced length of hospital stay and reduced health care cost.

Goals/Objective of Clinical Pharmacist Onward Round

• Investigate unusual drug orders or doses, checking drug chart.

• Detect adverse drug reactions and drug interactions

• Participate in patient discharge planning.

• Optimizes therapeutic management by influencing drug therapy selection, implementation, monitoring and follow up.

• It allows pharmacist to scc first how drugs are used and prescribed and to see the effects of these drugs on patients.

• Indenting medications as per drug chart

Classification of ward Round

        • Pre- rounds

        • Registrar/resident rounds

        • Professor/unit chief rounds

• Teaching rounds.

PREROUNDS

• Interns or post graduate students perform a daily review of patients in their unit ward.

• Learning opportunity to familiarize themselves with the cases.

• Trainee clinical pharmacist may join the intern or postgraduates in their prerounds and complete the patient medication and clinical review.

REGISTRAR/RESIDENT ROUNDS

• Registrar or resident individually of in a team conduct ward round at least once a day at a fixed time.

• These rounds are extensive and may also involve clinical teaching to medical postgraduate students and interns. –

• Useful rounds for clinical pharmacists of all level of experience to join.

PROFESSOR/UNIT CHIEF ROUNDS

• Unit / ward chief conducts the round together with their registrar, residents, postgraduate students and interns for all the patient under their care

• These rounds are extensive and address more complex issues regard and management.

• These rounds may be more challenging for clinical pharmacist in terms of their clinical knowledge.

TEACHING ROUNDS

• In teaching hospitals, academic medical staff conduct bedside clinical teaching rounds for residents, medical postgraduate students, interns and medical undergraduate students.

• Conducted few times a week

• This round provides opportunity for pharmacist to improve their clinical knowledge. Responsibility of clinical pharmacist during ward round

• Checking the Drug charts, dose, route, frequency

• Drug-Drug interaction

• Rectify the medication errors

• To monitor the patients' symptoms and side effects

• Drug-food interaction

2.TREATMENT CHART REVIEW

It is a fundamental responsibility of a pharmacist to ensure the appropriateness of medication orders.

It serves as starting point for other clinical pharmacy activities (medication counselling, TDM, DI, and ADR)

• Organizing information according to medical problems helps breakdown complex situation into its individual parts.

GOAL

• To optimize the patients drug therapy.

• To prevent or minimize drug related problems/medication errors

PROCEDURE

• The patients medical record should be reviewed in conjugation with medication administration record.

• Recent consultations, treatment plans and daily progress should be taken account when determining the appropriateness of current medication and planning each patient's care.

• Detecting orders for medication to which the patient may be hypersensitive intolerant

• The patient's previous medication order.

• Patient's specific considerations e.g. disease state, pregnancy.

• Drug dose and dosage schedule, especially with respect to age, renal function, liver function. • Route, dosage form and method of administration.

• Checking complete drug profile for medication duplication, interaction or incompatibilities. • Ensuring that administration times are appropriate e.g. with respect to food, other drug and procedures

• Reviewing medication for cost effectiveness

Components of Medication Order Review

Checking that medication order is written in accordance with legal and local requirements

✓Patient name and IP number

✓Age, gender

✓Drugs in capitals

✓Dose, ROA

✓Frequency

✓Duration of the treatment

✓Physician signature

✓Physician address and phone number

Identification of Drug Related Problems

✓ Untreated indication

✓ Inappropriate drug selection

✓ Sub therapeutic dose

✓ Adverse drug reaction

✓ Failure to receive drug

✓ Drug interactions

✓ Drug use without indication

✓ Over dosage

3.ADVERSE DRUG REACTION MONITORING

Any response to a drug which is noxious and unintended, and which occurs at doses normally used in man for prophylaxis, diagnosis or therapy of disease or for the modification of physiological function.

Classification of ADRs

Type A (Augmented)

Type B (bizarre)

Type C (chemical)

Type D (delayed)

Type E (exit/end of treatment)

Type F (familial)

Type G (genotoxicity)

Type U (Undefined)

Type A • Reactions which can be predicted from the known pharmacology of the drug.

• Dose dependent • Can be alleviated by a dose reduction.

• Example: - Anticoagulants- bleeding, Beta blockers - bradycardia, Nitrates-headache

Type B

• Cannot be predicted from the pharmacology of the drug

• Not dose dependent

•Host dependent factors important in predisposition

• Example: - Penicillin – Anaphylaxis, Anticonvulsant - Hypersensitivity

Type C

• Biological characteristics can be predicted from the chemical structure of the drug metabolite •

Example: - Paracetamol - hepatotoxicity

Type D

• Occur after many years of treatment

• Can be due to accumulation

- Example: - Chemotherapy - secondary tumors

- Phenytoin during pregnancy - teratogenic effects

- Antipsychotics - tardive dyskinesia

ADR MONITORING

- Identifying adverse drug reaction

- Assessing casualty (relationship between drug and suspected reaction)

- Documentation of ADR

- Reporting serious ADRs to pharmacovigilance centers / ADR regulating authorities

Documentation of Adrs

- Documents used for reporting ADRS

- Source documentation e.g. patients medical records, x-ray or diagnostic reports

- AE / SAE forms

- Paper case report form / electronic CRF

Reporting Serious ADRS

Information to be captured for reporting includes the following

- Patient details

- Initials

- Height

- Gender

- Age and date of birth

- Weight

4. DRUG INFORMATION

It is the current, relevant, critically examined data about drug and drug use for given patient or situation.

Many institutes run drug information center for the provision of drug information to every group/kind of people from any place.

Aims And Objective of Drug Information

- The provision of information to health profession specific the use of drugs particular patients. • The provision of information to officials in government agencies to optimize decision making process.

- To develop and participate in continuing education programs.

- To develop educational activities regarding the appropriate use of drugs for patients in the community

• To prepare and distribute material on drugs health personnel drug information bulletin or other media.

• To develop and participate in research programs.

• To improve patient compliance and to provide a guide to responsible self-medication

CLASSIFICATION OF DIC

✓ Hospital Based Dic

• Some of the major activities performed by hospital-based DIC include receiving and answering the in-house call by the requestor, involved in formulary decision making and providing service education, participating in drug use evaluation, publishing newsletter, reporting ADR, assist in investigational drug activity, and Pharmacy and Therapeutic Committee.

✓ Community-Based Dic

• Community-based DIC aims to change patient behaviour through drug therapy, improving patient adherence, thereby ultimately leads to quality health care.

The Functions of Dic

• Information on all aspects of therapeutic uses of drugs

• Information on dose and administration of drugs

• Information on drug - drug, drug-food and drug - herb interaction.

• Information on adverse effects of drugs

• Indication and safety indication of drugs

• Drugs in pregnancy and lactation.

• Availability / substitute, formulary decision etc.

• Drug information related to academic and research

• Continuous education programs for promoting rational use.

5. POISON INFORMATION CENTER

Poison information is a specialized area of drug information which includes information about the toxic effects of chemicals and pesticides, hazardous material spills, household products, overdose, of therapeutic medicines including mushrooms, animal toxins from snakes, spiders and other venomous creature and stings.

Types of Poison

Prescription drug

Over the counter drugs

Herbal medications or preparations

Household chemicals

Industrial chemicals

Poison Can Be

1. Unintentional poisoning

2. Intentional poisoning

- Drug overdose
- Suicide
- Drug abuse
- Murder
- Misreading of product labels
- Children

Functions

- Provision of information and advice
- Patient management
- Laboratory services
- Teaching and training
- Toxicovigilance
- Prevention

Provision of Information and Advice

• The main function of a poison information centre is to information and advice concerning the diagnosis, prognosis, treatment and prevention of poisoning, as well as about the toxicity of chemicals and the risks they pose.

Patient Management

• While a poison information center may have its own clinical toxicology unit or treatment facilities, poisoned patients may be cared for at any of a variety of medical facilities.

Laboratory Services

• A laboratory service for toxicological analyses and biomedical investigations is essential for the diagnosis, assessment and treatment of certain types of poisoning.

• The laboratory service can also determine the kinetics of the toxin, particularly its absorption, distribution, metabolism and elimination.

Teaching and training

• The experience gained in a poison information center can be an important source of human and animal toxicological data.

• The application and communication of this knowledge are vital for improving the prevention and management of poisoning centers thus have educational responsibilities that extend to training of medical practitioners and other professional health workers likely encounter cases of poisoning.

Toxicovigilance: is an essential function of poison information centres. It is the active process of identifying and evaluating the toxic risks existing in a community, and evaluating the measures taken to reduce or eliminate them.

Prevention

• Informing the general public, as well as special groups at risk, about recognized or emerging risks to the community posed by the use, transport, storage and disposal of specific chemicals and natural toxins, and giving guidance on how to avoid exposure to, or accidents with, these substances means such as brochures, leaflets, posters, educational programs, and campaigns in the media may be employed, but should not arouse unjustified false anxieties and should take due account of local psychosocial and cultural circumstances.

5. MEDICATION HISTORY

A medication history is a detailed, accurate and complete account of all prescribed and non-prescribed medications that a patient had taken or is currently taking prior to a initially institutionalized or ambulatory care

Goals

The information collected can be utilized to

1. Compare medication profile with the medication administration record an investigate the discrepancies.

2. Verify medication history taken by other staffs and provide additional information where appropriate

Information Sources

      1. Patient

      2. Family or care giver

      3. Medication vials/bubble packs

      4. Medication list

      5. Community pharmacy

      6. DPIN (Drug programs information network)

7. PATIENT COUNSELLING

Patient counselling refers to the process of providing information, advice and assistance to help patients use their medications appropriately.

• The information and advice are given by the pharmacist directly to the or to the patient's representative, and many also include information about the patient's illness or recommended lifestyle changes.

• During counselling, the pharmacist should assess the patient's understanding about his or her illness and the treatment, and provide individualized advice and information which will assist their medications in the patient to take their medications in the most safe and effective manner. • Good communication skills are required to gain the patient's confidence and to motivate the patient to adhere to the recommended regimen.

Objective

1. Patient should recognize the importance of medication for his well-being.

2.A working relationship and a foundation for continuous interaction and consultation should be established.

3.Patients understand strategies to deal with medication side effects and drug interactions should be improved.

4. Should ensure better patient compliance.

5. Patient becomes an informed, efficient and active participant in disease care management.

6.parmacist should be perceived as a professional who offers pharmaceutical care.

7.Drug interactions and adverse drug reactions should be prevented.

Communication Skills for Effective Counselling Counselling process uses following √**Verbal Communication**

- Language
- Tone
- Volume
- Rate of speed

√ **Nonverbal Communication**

- Body language
- Movement
- Proximity
- Eye contact
- Facial expression

Communication During Drug Therapy

- Purpose of medication
- How medication work

• Dose and duration of therapy

• Goals of therapy

• Adverse effect and how to deal with them

• Specific drug issues

Qualities of a Good Counsellor

• Be a good listener

• Be flexible • Be empathetic

• Be non-judgment

• Be tolerant

• Communicate confidently

Step During Patient Counselling

1. Preparing for the session

2. Opening of the session

3. Counselling content

4. Closing the session

1. Preparing for the Session

• The success of counselling depends on the knowledge and skill of counsellor.

• The pharmacists should know as much as possible about the patient and his/her treatment details.

• If the patient is receiving a medication which is unfamiliar to the pharmacist, then a drug information reference should be consulted before counselling commences.

2. Opening of the Session

• The first phase of counselling is used information gathering.

• The pharmacist should introduce him or herself the patient and greet them by name.

• It is the beat to use titles such as Ms., Mrs. and Mr. and then switch over to the fix name.

• The pharmacist should identify the purpose the session very clearly.

• During counselling, the pharmacist should avoid asking question in an embarrassing way, show excessive curiosity, discuss the patient problems, pass moral judgments, interrupt when the patient speaking, make is premature interpretations or argue with the patient.

3. Counselling Content

Topics commonly covered include

√ Name and strength of the medication.

√ The reason why it has been prescribed (if known), or how it works.

√ How to take the medication.

✓ Expected benefits of the treatment.

✓ Expected duration of the treatment.

✓ Possible adverse effects.

✓ Possible medications or dietary interactions.

✓ Advice on correct stage.

✓ Minimum duration required to Show therapeutic benefit.

✓ What to do if a dose is missed.

✓ Special monitoring requirements, for example, blood tests.

4. Closing the Session

• Before closing the session, it is essential to check the patient's understating

• This can be assessed by feedback questions, such as "Can you remember what this medication is for?" or for how long should you take this medication?" during the discussion some of the patient's information needs may have been cleared patient may have new questions or doubts. • Before final closure and if time permits, summarize the main points in logical order.

• If appropriate the pharmacist can supply their telephone number to encourage the patient to make contact if they need advice or information.

<h2 style="text-align:center">7.   INTERPROFESSIONAL COLLABORATION</h2>

• The process of developing and maintaining effective working relationships with learners, practitioners, patients /clients/families and communities to enable optimal health outcomes.

• Elements of collaboration include respect trust shared decision making an partnerships.

Roles And Responsibilities

• Know one's own role and those of team members

• Communicate team roles and responsibilities

• Engage diverse healthcare professionals to meet the needs of patients

• Use the full scope of knowledge, skill and abilities of available health professionals and health workers to provide safe, timely, efficient, effective and equitable care.

• Use respectful health care practices

Values And Ethics • Recognize and respect the unique cultures, values, roles / responsibilities and expertise of other health professions

• Work in cooperation with those who receive care, those who provide care, and contribute to or support the delivery of prevention and health care services.

• Place the interests of patients and populations at the centre of interprofessional health care delivery.

Communication

• Use respectful and appropriate communication in all situations

• Organize and communicate information with patients, families, and health care members in a form and format that is understandable, avoiding jargon.

• Listen actively and encourage ideas and opinions of all team members.

Teams and teamwork

• Work with others to deliver patient-centered, community responsive care.

• Engage when possible in shared patient- centered problem solving.

• Integrate knowledge and experience of other professions to inform effective decisions.

• Apply leadership and facilitation practices that support collaboration and team effectiveness.

Pharmaceutical Care Definition

• It is defined as the responsible provision of drug therapy for the purpose of achieving definite therapeutic outcomes that improve the patients quality of life.

• These outcomes are

√ Cure of the disease

√ Elimination or reduction of patient's symptomology

√ Arresting or slowing of a disease process

√ Preventing a disease or symptoms

• Pharmaceutical care involves the process through which a pharmacist cooperates with a patient and other professionals in designing, implementing and monitoring a therapeutic outcome for the patients

Drug Related Problems

- • Inappropriate prescription
- • Inappropriate delivery
- • Inappropriate patient behavior
- • Patient idiosyncrasy
- • Inappropriate monitoring and reporting
- • Lack of health literacy in the public.

Principle

• The principal elements of pharmaceutical care are that it is medication related; it is care that is directly provided to the patient; it is provided to produce definite outcomes; these outcomes are intended to improve the patient's quality of life; and the provider accepts personal responsibility for the outcomes.

Process of Pharmaceutical Care

- Collection of patient data
- Identification of problems
- Establishing outcomes goals through a good therapeutic plan or care plan.
- Evaluating treatment alternatives, by monitoring and modifying therapeutic plan.
- Individualizing drug regimens or drug interactions
- Monitoring outcomes

Purpose of Pharmaceutical Care Plan

- To determine, with the patient how to manage medical conditions or illnesses successfully with Pharmacotherapy
- Patient counselling
- Pharmaceutical service

Function of Pharmaceutical Care Plan

- A redesign of the professional work flow
- Assignment of technical functions to technical personnel under the direct supervision and Responsibility of the pharmacist.
- In pharmaceutical care, care plans are organized by indications for drug therapy.
- Patients often have multiple medical conditions.
- Some conditions are acute and many are chronic requiring long-term treatment.

Pharmaceutical care interventions are

- To initiate new drug therapy
- To resolve and prevent drug therapy problems
- Patient education
- Each pharmaceutical care plan must address the need to prevent the development of new drug therapy problems.
- In clinical practice design drug therapies and patient education to avoid preventable side effects or risks known to be associated with certain drug therapies or diseases.

Medication Therapy Management

- A range of services provided to individual patients to optimize therapeutic outcomes and detect and prevent costly medication problems
- MTM provided by pharmacists, the medication therapy expert, results in:

✓ A review of all medications prescribed by all prescribers providing care to the patient, and any over the counter and herbal products the patient may be taking to identify and address medication problems.

✓ Problems may include medications, not being used correctly, duplication of medication unnecessary medications, and the need for medication for an untreated or inappropriately managed condition.

✓ In depth, medication related education, consultation and advice provided to patients, family or caregivers to help assure proper use of medications.

Home Medication Review

• Home Medication Review (HMR) is 'a service designed to assist consumers living at home to maximize the benefit of their medication regimen & prevent medication related problems.

• It is a consumer-focused, structured and collaborative service offered to consumer living at home in the community.

•HMR involves a team approach, with the consumer, their general practitioner, their pharmacy, and other relevant members of the health care team in a comprehensive review of medications in the home setting

Objective

The specific objectives of HMR are

• To increase patients' adherence to medication and patients' knowledge on medication

• To identify factors affecting non-compliance

• To review patients' method of managing their medication at home

• To reduce wastage (due to overstocking of medicine)

• To improve patient's quality of life.

Process Of HMR

• Process of HMR involves following steps

✓ Consumer identification

✓ General practitioner

✓ Consumer consent

✓ HMR interview

✓ HMR report medication management

✓ Plan follow up

OVER THE COUNTER (OTC) SALES

OTC drugs are those drugs which are safe and effective for use by the general public without a doctor's prescription.

It is also called prescription de controlled drugs.

These drugs are the non-prescription or over-the-counter drugs.

These have little significant pharmacological activity and therefore the physician need not to be very much concerned about their use by the patients themselves.

It is used primarily for symptomatic relief and not as substitutes for prescription drugs.

Significance

Comparatively cheaper

Chemist himself may prescribe OTC

Consumers are able to

Self-diagnose

Self-treat

Self-manage

OTC considered as time saving medications. Some patients do not want to spend much time at physician's clinic.

Lesser number of side effect compared to prescription medications. Drugs Used by Indians

Over-the-counter drug products account for 55 percent of drugs used by Indians, whereas Prescription Drugs account for 45 percent

Types Of OTC Medications

☐ Analgesics ☐ Antibiotics ☐ Cough Suppressants ☐ Anti Acne Drugs ☐ NSAIDS ☐ Antiseptics ☐ Decongestants ☐ Antacids ☐ Antifungals ☐ Anti Histamines ☐ Smoking Cessation Drugs

Rules For the Proper Use of OTC Drugs

Always know what you are taking.

Know the effects.

Read and heed the warnings and cautions.

Don't use anything for more than 1 to 2 wks.

Be particularly cautious if also taking prescription drugs.

If you have questions, ask a pharmacist. ☐ If you don't need it, don't use it!

Special Patient Groups

☐ Many patient groups may be particularly susceptible to adverse events that are caused by OTC products. They include:

    ☐ Children

    ☐ Women who are pregnant or breast feeding

    ☐ Geriatric patients

    ☐ People taking prescription drugs & people having health problems

Otc Medications Are Safe but Not Risk-Free

- As with all medications, there can be risks with use.
- The risks of OTC use include: Delay in seeking medical advice for a serious illness. Risk of drug-drug/herbal/dietary supplement interactions. Risk of adverse events. Potential for dependence, misuse and abuse.

Misuse And Abuse of OTC Drugs

☐ Physical dependence

☐ Psychological dependence

☐ Nonprescription products that can be severely habit-forming: decongestants, laxatives, antihistamines, sleep aids, antacids and ephedrine.

☐ Only 16% reads the entire product label.

☐ If they read them they do not follow the directions on the label.

☐ Abuse is most common in adolescents aged 10-17 years.

☐ Adolescents are 18% times more likely to die from an OTC overdose than from a illicit drug dose overdose.

Rational Use of OTC Drugs

☐ Rational use of medicines refers to the correct, proper and appropriate use of medicines.

☐ Rational use requires that patients receive the appropriate medicine, in the proper dose, for an adequate period of time and at the lowest cost.

ANALGESICS

☐ Pain relief medicines (also known as "analgesics" and "painkillers") are regulated by the Food and Drug Administration (FDA).

☐ Some analgesics, including opioid analgesics, act on the body's peripheral and central nervous systems to block or decrease sensitivity to pain.

☐ Others act by inhibiting the formation of certain chemicals in the body.

☐ These relieve the minor aches and pains associated with conditions such as headaches, fever, colds, flu, arthritis, toothaches, and menstrual cramps.

☐ There are basically two types of OTC pain relievers: 1. Acetaminophen 2. Non-steroidal anti-inflammatory drugs (NSAIDs).

☐ Acetaminophen is an active ingredient found in more than 600OTC and prescription medicines, including pain relievers, cough suppressants, and cold medications.

☐ NSAIDs are common medications used to relieve fever and minor aches and pains.

☐ They include aspirin, naproxen, and ibuprofen, as well as many medicines taken for colds, sinus pressure, and allergies.

☐ They act by inhibiting an enzyme that helps make a specific chemical.

Use as Directed

☐ Pain medications are safe and effective when used as directed. However, misuse of these products can be extremely harmful and even deadly.

☐ Consumers who take pain relief medications must follow their health care professional's instructions carefully. If a measuring tool is provided with your medicine, use it as directed.

☐ Do not change the dose of your pain relief medication without talking to your doctor first. ☐ Also, pain medications should never be shared with anyone else. Only your health care professional can decide if a prescription pain medication is safe for someone.

Special Patient Groups

☐ Talk with your doctor before taking any NSAID if you:

☐ Are over age 60 ☐ Are pregnant or nursing

☐ Have three or more drinks of alcohol every day

☐ Have bleeding problems

☐ Have liver or kidney disease

☐ Have heart disease

☐ Take a medicine to thin the blood, such as warfarin (Coumadin)

☐ Take a medicine for high blood pressure

☐ Children and teenagers who are recovering from a viral infection such as the flu or chickenpox should not take aspirin. It has been linked to Reye's syndrome, a serious but rare condition that can result in brain, kidney, and liver damage.

☐ Naproxen sodium is not recommended for children under 2.

☐ Ibuprofen is considered safe for children 6 months and older in the right dose.

OTC Counselling Questions

Counselling patients about self-care and nonprescription drugs is not the same and cannot follow the same procedure as for prescription drugs.

That is why OTC counselling requires much more exploratory open or close- ended questions on the part of the pharmacist which are especially useful to clarify information gathered about the patient's condition.

It allows gathering the most abundant amount of information.

These questions usually start with who, what, how, why or where. For example:

> ? "Which of the prescription medications do you take on regular basis?"
>
> ? "Which of the nonprescription and herbal medications do you use?"
>
> ? "What types of conditions do you routinely see your doctor for
>
> ?" Some other questions are also possible:
>
> ? "Have you ever experienced any side effects after taking the OTC medication?"
>
> ? "Have you taken this OTC medication before?"

Patient Counselling

Step 1

- Every pharmacist should begin the OTC counselling session by introducing himself/herself by name which identifies him/her as the pharmacist.
- He/she should try to relax the patient by beginning the session with a friendly smile and a handshake.
- The pharmacist should also explain that he/she can provide assistance with OTC product selection and explain how to use such medication.

Step 2

- In order to elicit key information, the pharmacist should first and foremost try to obtain relevant information about patient's demographic (e.g. sex, age, pregnant, nursing, weight, allergies, social history etc), disease (e.g. history of present illness, current symptoms, course of illness, past history, other underlying medical conditions) and drug (e.g. current medication, medication taking history, OTC history etc.)
- Moreover, by using suitable verbal and written communication techniques, the pharmacist should inform, educate, and counsel patients about the following:
- Drug name (generic and/or brand name)
- Route, dosage form, dosage and administration schedule;
- Special directions for preparation and administration as well as precautions to be taken during the process;

- Techniques for self-monitoring of drug therapy;
- Storage;
- Potential drug-drug or drug-food interactions or other therapeutic contraindications; and
- Accordingly other Information "peculiar to the specific patient or drug etc.
- In addition, it is of vital importance to demonstrate to patient's- how to use medications in various forms such as inhalers, patches, drops, ointments, lozenges, gargles etc.
- And ask them to demonstrate making sure that patients understand which route of administration should be used thus ensuring that patients have all the necessary instructions in writing and that they understand how to schedule their medications in accordance with meals and other medications.

DRUG STORE/PHARMACY/COMMUNITY PHARMACY/CHEMIST'S

A retail shop which provides prescription drugs, among other products.

At the drug store, a pharmacist oversees the fulfilment of medical prescriptions & is available to give advice on their offerings of over-the- counter drugs.

A typical pharmacy would be in the commercial area of a community. • Every hospital should have a medical store for the purpose of procuring, stocking & distributing the drugs and medicines to various departments.

ORGANISATION OF DRUG STORE

Stores are defined as a sub-organisation in any hospitals where materials obtained are held in abeyance till inspected, approved and stocked.

A store should have a standard specification of materials and since the store procured the drugs on behalf of the department for regular flow of material, the condition of storage should be proper.

OBJECTIVES OF DRUG STORES

1. To stock all drugs and accessories required in the hospital.

2. To procure drugs from different sources.

3. To supply drugs to the consuming departments.

4. To store drugs required in research work.

5. To preserve records of receipt and issue of drugs.

6. To maintain records of receipt and issue of drugs.

7. To carry out all operations regarding drugs economically to save revenue

LAYOUT OF DRUG STORE

Preferably located on the ground floor close to the pharmacy.

Area: at least 600-1000 sq ft.

Adequate storage facilities to avoid deterioration of the drugs, chemicals, biological etc. by moisture or heat.

An ideal store:

02entrances, one for receiving the articles and other for issue of materials.

Racks: for storage of material made of angled iron, having partitions.

Costly items are stored in closed bins.

The height of racks depends up on the height of ceiling & should be above 2/3rd the height.

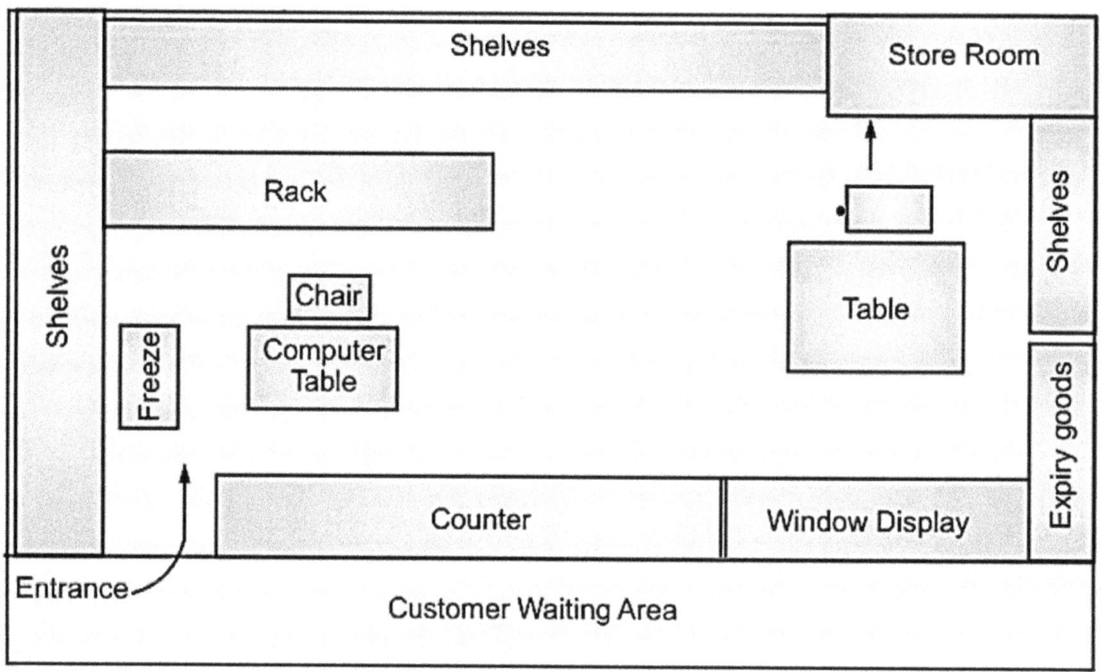

Layout of Retail Pharmacy Store

RETAIL DRUG STORE DESIGN

DRUG STORE

A definite location code is to be followed in order to identify the product or material placed in store.

For this purpose, following system may be adapted:

(i)   F S N- Fast moving, slow moving, non moving

(ii)   H M L- Heavy, medium, light materials

Fast moving materials are placed near the issue exit while

Non-moving articles are placed far from the exit.

Heavy items are placed at the bottom & light items on the top.

DRUG STORE....

Records are maintained using Bin Card system.

A ledger or bin card has 4 codes like-

1 2 3 4 (1-Panel, 2-Row, 3-Rack, 4-Bin)

A 5 B 3

This means panel A, 5th row, Rack B and Bin 3

Materials can be entered either in ledger or bin cards in Alphabetical order but this may cause problems as number of drugs are known buy different name.

They may be categorised & stored depending up on their therapeutic effect.

TYPES OF MATERIALS STOCKED

Sufficient number of racks should be provided for storage of drugs & supplies.

CO2 fire extinguishers at strategic points along with fire buckets to fight sudden fires due to stored drugs & chemical.

Stocked Materials are:

(i)   Capsules, tablets, liquid dosage form & injections etc.

(ii)   Biological antibiotics in refrigerator.

(iii)   Narcotic & psychotropic substances stored under lock & key.

(iv)   POISOINS are stored in separate closed rack, labelled as "POISION".

(v)   Alcohol & alcohol containing preparations.

(vi)   Large bulk items on bottom.

(vii)   Vaccines & other thermolabile drugs @ cold store (2-10°C). Antibiotics, vitamins liver preparations @ at cool temp (15-20°C).

(viii) To avoid pilferage, store costly drugs & prescribed schedule X drugs separately under lock & key.

STORAGE CONDITIONS

Condition	Temperature
Cold storage	2-8°C
Cool temp	8-25°C
Room temp RT-temp	Temperature prevailing in working area
Warm	30-40°C
Excessive Heat	Above 40°C

COLD STORAGE (2-8°C)

A separate room or a portion should be maintained at this temp range.

Should have a recording thermometer & temp should be noted at least twice daily.

It should remain under the supervisor & in case a separate room is not available, adequate number of refrigerators should be provided for the purpose.

The maintenance of these refrigerators in working order is the responsibility of the supervisor.

Drugs: insulin, sera, whole human blood, frozen plasma, thromboplastin, oxytocin injection, and certain vaccines etc. are not allowed to freeze.

The chief pharmacist should personally check that such drugs are stored at respective places as per their prescribed storage conditions.

LIST A – (DRUGS REQUIRING COLD STORAGE 2-8OC)

1. Sera   2. Vaccines   3. Whole human blood   4. Concentrated human red blood corpuscles(4-6oC)   5. Normal human plasma   6. Frozen plasma –at a temp not above -18oC   7. Thrombin   8. Thromboplastin   9. Cobra venom in solution   10. Viper venom in solution   11. Posterior pituitary injection   12. Oxytocin injection   13. Vasopressin injection   14. Corticotropin gelatin injection   15. Corticotrophin zinc oxide injection   16. Cholistin sulphamethate injection   17. Suxamethonium chloride injection   18. Insulin preparation   19. Human gamma globulin injection   20. Normal liquid human serum albumin   21. Schick test toxin

STORAGE AT COOL TEMPERATURE (8-25°C)

The space of this room should be adequate considering the maximum stock of drugs likely to be purchased by the hospital during any time of the year.

The chief pharmacist should ensure that no drug falling in this category is stocked away from this room.

An inspection register should be maintained by the Chief pharmacist.

Examples: antibiotics, vitamins, liver preparations.

LIST – B (DRUGS REQUIRING STORAGE AT COOL TEMP. 8-25OC)

Antibiotics preparations   • Crystalline penicillin   • Potassium phenoxy methyl penicillin   • Benzethine penicillin   • Cloxacillin   • Methicillin • Ampicillin   • Streptomycin sulphate and chloride   • Tetracycline, oxytetracycline, chlortetracycline   • Bacitracin and zinc bacitracin Others   • Dextran injection • Dextran sulphate injection • Dextrose injection • Dextrose and sodium injection • Heparin injection BP • Hyaluronidase injection • Chlorambucin preparations • Chorhexidine • Choline theophyline preparation • Liver injection crude • Ergot liquid extract. Arsenicals (inj) • Neoarsphenamine • Sulpharsphenamine • Tryprsanide Blood Preparations (-below 20°C) • Dried plasma • Human fibrin foam • Human fibrinogen • Human serum dried • Human thrombin Hormone preparations • Corticotropin • Betamethasone sodium phosphate injection • Chorionic gonadotropin • Prednisolone sodium phosphate injection • Oxytocin tablets Vitamin preparations • Preparation containing vit. A, vit. B1, vit.B2, vit.B6, vit.C, vit.D • Vit. B complex elixir and injection • Vit. K injection • Vit. K preparations

PURCHASE AND INVENTORY CONTROL

Basic purpose of purchases:

To ensure continuous flow of raw materials of right quality, right quantity, right price and from right sources.

Objective of purchasing: Avoidance of duplication & wastage with respect to various items purchased.

Centralized purchase by medical stores procures the drugs on behalf of all the departments & helps in getting quality drugs at cheaper rates.

Some important terms:

1.Right Quality - the quality which is available according to the particulars mentioned in terms of grades, brands or trade name, physico-chemical characteristics, etc. The quality must describe even the national standards to the extent it is possible.

2. Right Quantity - an important parameter of purchasing for continuous supply of raw materials. "Economic order Quantity" or any other technique may be followed in order to avoid shortage.

3. Right Price - consistent matching with the quality of drug. Generally tender system is followed in hospitals & the lowest bidder is chosen for supplying the order.

4. Right Source -The supplier should be dependable & capable of supplying as per requirements from time to time. The selection of supplier requires consideration of various factors.

5. Right Time -Purchase department should have lead time information for all products. Lead time: Total time period between the placing of order & receipt of material while doing purchases. The purchase committee should consider emergency situations like floods, strikes, accidents, etc. Some important terms

PURCHASE PROCEDURE

Steps for procurement of goods:

I. Determination of Requirement- The materials to be purchased for particular period are well planned for the purpose of their regular and continuous use. Purchase requisition is generally prepared by departmental heads & provides information mentioned below.

(a) Type of material to be purchased,

(b) Time of requirement,

(c) Quantity to be purchased,

    II. Source of Supply- The pharmacy and therapeutic committee sets adequate standards for the purchase of quality drugs. Procurement of stores is generally done by following sources:

    (i)   Medical store depot

    (ii)   Directorate general supplies and disposals

    (iii)   Direct from wholesalers and manufacturers

    (iv)   By inviting tenders

    (v)   Emergency purchases from local market

    (i)   **Medical Store Depot (MSD).**

This organisation has 06 medical store deport: Mumbai, Chennai, Calcutta, karnal, Hyderabad, Guwahati.

The purchased items are subjected to various in-house tests at the testing units in Chennai and Mumbai.

It runs on no-profit & no-loss basis.

(ii)   **Directorate General Supplies and Disposals (DGS &D)**

DGS&D calls for tender and places the order. The payment is made only after the verification of inspection report by the indentor on the prescribed Performa.

(iii)   **Direct Purchase from Whole sellers or Manufacturer**

Direct purchases from whole sellers, manufacturers are done following a proper purchase procedure. Materials are then received and stocked at their relevant places under proper storage conditions.

(iv)   **By Inviting tenders**

Tenders are invited from various supplier and generally the lowest bidder is chosen for supplying the order. However, price and quality both are considered as well.

(iv)   **Emergency drugs from local market**

Items not available at MSD, DGS & D and any emergency drug which is out of stock can be immediately purchased from local market. For this purchase form is prepared in duplicate, one copy is sent to the department & other copy is retained in the pharmacy.

This avoids the department concerned to re-order the same item.

III. Purchase Order-

After selecting the supplier, the chief pharmacist or any other suitable authority prepares a purchase order giving detailed description, specification, packaging, price and quantity needed etc. of the items.

This purchase order is in written form and it is the evidence of contract between the buyer and the supplier.

Number of purchase order copies varies from hospitals to hospital.

(a) The original copy is sent to the supplier.

(b) One copy for accounts section.

(c) One copy for purchase department.

(d) One copy for the department.

(e) Fifth and Sixth copy for concerned receiving department.

(f) Seventh copy as history copy.

The purchase order should clearly indicate the terms and conditions, i.e., price, quality, and time of delivery. There should be a regular follow-up of purchase order so that drugs and supplies can be received timely.

PURCHASE REQUEST FORM

PURCHASE REQUEST

Date

Department

Vendor #	
Company	
Address	
City ___ State ___ Zip ___
Telephone ___ Fax ___

PURCHASE REQUESTS
MUST
BE APPROVED
BEFORE A
PURCHASE ORDER WILL
BE ISSUED

REQUESTED BY	PHONE	DEPARTMENT	JOB OR ACCOUNT NO.	PREVIOUS SUPPLIER ☐ Yes ☐ No

QUANTITY	ITEM NUMBER	ITEM TO BE PURCHASED	UNIT PRICE	TOTAL
			TOTAL	

PURCHASING DEPARTMENT USE ONLY	
DATE ORDERED	P.O. NUMBER
APPROVED BY	

General terms and conditions

-Deliveries must be made inside the hospital premises.

-Prepare all transport charges.

-The hospital will not be responsible for goods supplied which are not on this order form, not duly signed by the purchase officer.

-All consignments are subject to inspection.

-Installation and Demonstration, if required, is essential.

-No packing, forwarding or any other charges will be paid extra

IV. Receipt of Acknowledgment-

After placing the order to supplier by sending a copy of purchase order, the supplier in turn sends acknowledgement of the order saying that he will be able to supply the goods with the terms and conditions which are mentioned in the purchase order.

V. Receipt of Drugs-

On receipt of drugs, there should be a system in the stores whereby the supply of drugs received in the medical stores from the manufacturer are properly checked person specially assigned for this purpose.

Preferably the same person is responsible for reviewing the stocks, date of expiry, description, quantity, batch number, as mentioned in the order form.

Random sampling can be done to make sure that products confirm to the tendered specifications like date of expiry and visible sign of deterioration, such as change of colour, caking etc.

If any such deterioration is observed the matter should be reported to medical superintendent and local drug inspector. These stocks should never be used until the drug inspector's permission is granted and even the information should be sent to the manufacturer.

After the thorough examination of drugs, the above officer should give "No objection to accept the supply" in writing on the hospital copies of delivery challans, Invoices by putting signature and date. The invoice received from the supplier is sent to accounts section for accuracy along with price and quantity. After verification, the accounts section certifies and passes, the invoice for payment and on this basis, cashier makes the payment either by cheque/draft.

VI. Distribution of Drugs to Wards- Drugs should be supplied in the original packing of manufacturers.

However, if it is not possible to do so, then that should be supplied in clean containers so that the integrity and original properties can be preserved.

Name and quantity of the drug should be properly labelled. It is always advisable that suitable precautions should be taken to dispose of "Original empty containers" in order to avoid their misuse. The containers should be destroyed in the presence of a responsible person with a written statement signed by him.

Chief pharmacist should visit wards to check whether the drugs are properly stored under special storage conditions like cold storage, cool temperature and at room temperature.

INVENTORY CONTROL

Drug store management is based on principles of inventory control. mismanagement of stores & non-applicability of Scientific & Modern techniques has been identified as the root cause of material storage in majority of hospitals.

Objective of Inventory Control

    (i)   To supply drug in time.

    (ii)   To reduce investment in inventories and made effective use of capital investment.

    (iii)   Efforts are made to procure goods at minimum price without bargaining the quality.

    (iv)   To avoid stock out and shortage.

    (v)   Wastage are avoided.

TECHNIQUES OF INVENTORY CONTROL / METHODS USED FOR ANALYSIS OF DRUG EXPENDITURE

    (i)   ABC analysis

    (ii)   (ii) VED analysis

    (iii)   (iii) EOQ

    (iv)   (iv) Lead time

    (v)   (v) Buffer stock

(i)   ABC analysis

An inventory categorization technique.

It is a basic tool with a selective approach for concentration upon the items. As ABC analysis the items are divided into three categories—

"A items" with very tight control and accurate records,

"B items" with less tightly controlled and good records, and

"C items" with the simplest controls possible and minimal records.

The ABC analysis provides a mechanism for identifying items that will have a significant impact on overall inventory cost, while also providing a mechanism for identifying different categories of stock that will require different management & controls.

- The ABC analysis suggests that inventories of an organization are not of equal value. Inventory is grouped into three categories (A, B, and C) in order of their estimated importance.

- 'A' items are very important for an organization. Because of the high value of these 'A' items, frequent value analysis is required. In addition to that, an organization needs to choose an appropriate order pattern (e.g. 'just-in-time') to avoid excess capacity. 'B' items are important, but of course less important than 'A' items and more important than 'C' items. Therefore, 'B' items are intergroup items. 'C' items are marginally important.

• There are no fixed thresholds for each class, & different proportions can be applied based on objectives & criteria. ABC Analysis is similar to the Pareto principle in that the 'A' items will typically account for a large proportion of the overall value, but a small percentage of the number of items.

Examples of ABC class are

• 'A' items – 20% of the items accounts for 70% of the annual consumption value of the items • 'B' items – 30% of the items accounts for 25% of the annual consumption value of the items • 'C' items – 50% of the items accounts for 5% of the annual consumption value of the items Another recommended breakdown of ABC classes:

• "A" approximately 10% of items or 66.6% of value

• "B" approximately 20% of items or 23.3% of value

• "C" approximately 70% of items or 10.1% of value

(ii)   VED analysis is an inventory management technique that classifies inventory based on its functional importance. It categorizes stock under three heads based on its importance and necessity for an organization for production or any of its other activities. VED analysis stands for Vital, Essential, and Desirable.

V- Vital Category

Includes inventory, which is necessary for production or any other process in an organization. The shortage of items under this category can severely hamper or disrupt the proper functioning of operations. Hence, continuous checking, evaluation, and replenishment happen for such stocks. If any of such inventories are unavailable, the entire production chain may stop. Also, a missing essential component may be of need at the time of a breakdown. Therefore, order for such inventory should be before- hand. Proper checks should be put in place by the management to ensure the continuous availability of items under the "vital" category.

E- Essential category

Includes inventory, which is next to being vital. These, too, are very important for any organization because they may lead to a stoppage of production or hamper some other process. But the loss due to their unavailability may be temporary, or it might be possible to repair the stock item or part.The management should ensure optimum availability and maintenance of inventory under the "Essential" category too. The unavailability of inventory under this category should not cause any stoppage or delays.

D- Desirable Category

It is the least important among the three, & their unavailability may result in minor stoppages in production or other processes. Moreover, the easy replenishment of such shortages is possible in a short duration of time.

(iii)   Economic order quantity (EOQ)

The ideal order quantity a company should purchase to minimize inventory costs such as holding costs, shortage costs, & order costs. The formula assumes that demand, ordering, and holding costs all remain constant.

Formula and Calculation of EOQ

$$EOQ = \sqrt{\frac{2 * F * D}{I * C}} = \sqrt{\frac{2 * F * D}{H}}$$

$$EOQ = \sqrt{\frac{2 * Fixed\ Cost\ to\ Purchase * Demand\ Per\ Time}{Inventory\ Carrying\ Cost\ Per\ Unit\ Per\ Time}}$$

Usually the 'Unit of Time' is ANNUALLY, therefore

$$EOQ = \sqrt{\frac{2 * Fixed\ Cost\ to\ Purchase * Annual\ Demand}{Annual\ Inventory\ Carrying\ Cost\ Per\ Unit}}$$

six-sigma-material.com

- The goal of the EOQ formula is to identify the optimal number of product units to order. If achieved, a company can minimize its costs for buying, delivery, and storing units. Formula can be modified to determine different production levels or order intervals, & corporations with large supply chains and high variable costs use an algorithm in their computer software to determine EOQ.

- EOQ is an important cash flow tool. The formula can help a company control the amount of cash tied up in the inventory balance. For many companies, inventory is its largest asset other than its human resources, and these businesses must carry sufficient inventory to meet the needs of customers. If EOQ can help minimize the level of inventory, the cash savings can be used for some other business purpose or investment.

- The EOQ formula determines a company's inventory reorder point. When inventory falls to a certain level, the EOQ formula, if applied to business processes, triggers the need to place an order for more units. By determining a reorder point, the business avoids running out of inventory and can continue to fill customer orders. If the company runs out of inventory, there is a shortage cost, which is the revenue, lost because the company has insufficient inventory to fill an order. An inventory shortage may also mean the company loses the customer or the client will order less in the future.

(iv)   Lead time

The lead time is the sum of the supply delay & the reordering delay.

The lead time is the applicable duration to calculate the lead demand, the safety stock or the reorder point through a direct quantile forecast.

The longer the lead time, the higher the total inventory level or the larger is the safety stock, resulting in excess of investment in inventories.

As far as possible efforts should be made to decrease the lead time for effective inventory control.

(V) Buffer stock

Buffer stock is used in emergency to meet the unforeseen demands/ it refers to minimum quantity of a particular item which must be kept in the stores of all time. Buffer stocks can be calculated using the following formula;

• Buffer stocks= (Maximum consumption rate/day average- consumption rate/day) X lead time • Buffer stocks need following factors to be taken into consideration like;

    (i)   Lead time

    (ii)   Nature of item and rate of consumption

    (iii)   Availability of substitutes

    (iv)   Re-order level

    (v)   Stock out cost

Modern Computerization of Inventory Control

• National information centre (NIC) is working hard to prepare software which would facilitate proper control of inventory through the implementation of accepted principles of material management such as ABC analysis, "Last is the first out" etc. It would minimize the chances of validity of drugs expiring while in storage by the transfer of stocks from the surplus to deficit depots.

• Computerization will serve following purposes:

    (i)   Less investment

    (ii)   Less storage

    (iii)   Fast supply of drug

    (iv)   Control on Issue of Drugs

    (v)   Minimum wastage

    (vi)   Prompt payments

Reorder Level

• The reorder level is the level of the stock of a particular item, held by the firm, when an order is needed to be placed for avoiding the risk of being out of stock. It is based on the average time taken by the supplier for replenishment, maximum usage of the item during the replenishment time, & safety stock requirement. It is also known as reorder point. Reorder level is the stock level of a particular item of inventory, at which a firm needs to place an order for the fresh supply or replenishment of the item. It gives a signal regarding when to place a new order for the fresh supply of an inventory item.

- The internal factors involved in reorder level are maximum usage during the lead time, safety level, & replenishment period. Whereas the external factor involved in reorder level is lead time taken by the supplier. The main risk factor in reorder level is being out of stock & some other risk factors are disruption in production & foregone sales.

- Formula for estimation of reorder level: Reorder level = (Average daily usage rate x Average lead time in days) + Safety level

INVESTIGATIONAL USE OF DRUGS

Investigational drugs are those drugs or mixture or chemical which are not released and certified by the food and drug administration for the general use and sale for commercial concern. These drugs usually stand the statement on their labels as 'caution: New Drug- limited by federal law to investigational use" they are released only to principle investigator who is the member of medical staff of hospital after obtaining consent by duly sign the food and drug release for the manufacture of respective investigational drugs.

Principle

Hospital are the primary centres for clinical investigational on drug.

Investigational drug should be used only under the direct supervision of the principle investigator who should be member of medical staff and who should assumed the burden of securing the necessary consent.

When nurses are called upon to administer investigational drug they should have available to them basic information concerning such drugs including dosage form strength available, action and uses, side effect and symptoms of toxicity etc.

Classification of investigational new drug

Class A: • This class should contain all investigational use drugs which are under the preliminary experiment stage.

These drugs are restricted to use only by principle investigator.

Class B: • This class of investigational drug has passed through preliminary experimental research stage. In this class the investigational drugs are supplied to pharmacy department by principle investigator and are only dispensed after obtaining of his written prescription which duly sign.

Class C: • This class of investigational use of drug approved by the USP, NF, or passed by the federal FDA for use and sale as commercial concern. These drugs may be used only in hospital setup for their patient under the supervision of medical staff after fulfillment of specific procedure

Class D: • These classes of drug have been accepted for use in hospital and are listed in the hospital formulary.

Classification on the basis of Pharmacy operation

(a) General: An FDA approved drugs which as recommended as essential for good patient care with a well-established usage once accepted may be prescribed by all members of attending and house staff.

(b) Conditional: certain drugs may be approved for a conditional period of trail. A drug approved by FDA for general use but which the committee wishes to evaluate for given period before final consideration. May be prescribed by all member of the attending and house staff. (c) Investigational: Drug which are not approved by the FDA for use other than under controlled clinical setting must be approved by the Research advisory committee. A Protocol of any study involving drug must be submitted by the pharmacy.

Advisory committee and their responsibilities

- In the view of drug which are used in the investigational purpose in the hospital are subjected to review by advisory committee which are nothing by the committee on the human use in research and pharmacy and therapeutic committee (PTC) in which the principle investigator should provide all the information related to investigational drug to the PTC and should letter for intention to use of investigational drug in patient.
- It is the responsibilities of hospital and member of PTC to develop procedure and policies for holding of investigational drugs in the hospital for patient benefits.

Control of investigational use of drug

All investigational drug should be registered with the pharmacy and therapeutic committee. This may be accomplished bay a latter from the principle investigator, which provide the following information.

1. New drug name
2. Generic Name
3. Manufacturer
4. Chemical name
5. Proprietary Name
6. General chemistry
7. Pharmacology
8. Toxicology
9. Dose Range
10. Method of Administration
11. Antidote
12. Therapeutic uses

In order to control the use of investigational drugs many pharmacists have developed various forms which may be used to disseminate the above information on an investigational use drug to the various staff doctors and nurses.

The forms are usually titled.

1. Physician's data sheet on investigational drug

2. Nurses data sheet on investigational drug

3. Pharmacist data sheet on investigational drug.

1.Physician's data sheet

1) name of investigational drug

2) Manufacturer

3) Strength/ Dosage forms

4) Amount Received

5) Date received.

6) Control or Batch

7) Pharmacology and therapeutic properties, Dosage, Precaution.

8) Mode of Administration.

9) Signature of investigator

2. Nurses Data sheet

1) Name of investigational drug

2) Manufacturer

3) Strength and form

4) Pharmacology and therapeutic properties, dosage, and precaution.

5) Mode of administration.

 6) Signature of Nursing in charge.

Pharmacist data sheet.

Pharmacist's Data Sheet

Investigational Drug:--------   Manufacture:------

Chief Investigator: ---------------------

Date	Physician	Patient	Rx.#	Amount	Ward
------	-------------	----------	-----	-----------	--------
-----	-------------	----------	-----	-----------	--------

Authorization for Treatment with drug under clinical investigation.

The law department of American medical association states that drug under clinical investigation should be administered only were.

1. The informed consent of the patient or his/her authorized representative has been obtained. 2. The Physician is convinced of the reasonable accessory of his diagnosis and, if necessary, has confirmed it by adequate consultation and

3. Existing method of treatment have proven unsatisfactory.

Role of Pharmacist in clinical investigation of drug

- During this stage the pharmacist can play an important role by assisting in the development of the protocol and the control of double-blind test/study having the experimental drug or placebo prepared exactly the same dosage forms and presentation. Neither the present nor the doctor informed as to whether the placebo and the potent article.

- Collecting, storing and distributing essential information concerning the drug being studied. Packing and labelling investigational drug in multiple or unit dosage containers.

- Preparing dosage forms

- Dispensing of investigational drug to both inpatient or outpatient

Advisory committee for the investigational use of drug.

1. The Pharmacy and Therapeutic Committee

2. FDA Advisory Committee System.

1) The pharmacy and therapeutic committee (PTC)

• The PTC is a group of people which formulate policies regarding evaluation and therapeutic use of investigational drug.

• The committee is composed of physician, Pharmacist and other health care professionals with the inclusion of medical staff.

• It looks after the safety in handling and administering the investigational drug.

• It also plays a vital role in monitoring adverse drug reaction. Every case of adverse drug reaction is first reported by the attending physician to the chairman of the PTC.

• The PTC interact with the various government bodies like (DTAB) central drug institute (Lucknow) Drug controller central of India. AIMS (New Delhi) PGI Chandigarh for consultation of adverse drug reaction of investigational drug.

2 FDA advisory committee system

• FDA advisory committee provide technical assistance related to the development and evaluation of investigational drug. Biologics and medical device.

• The primary role of FDA advisory committee is to provide independent expert scientific advice to the agency in its evaluation of investigational drug any stage of consideration by the agency.

INTERPRETATION OF CLINICAL LABORATORY TESTS

Clinical laboratory test results are a very important parameter in diagnosis monitoring and screening. 70-80 % of decisions in diagnosis are based on laboratory results and more and more laboratory analyses are requested. Thus, a lot of data are provided and that is therefore imperative for patient care (and safety) that the clinicians are familiar with the tests and with interpretation of the results.

The laboratory result must be interpreted on the background of a reference interval that is used to distinguish between "health" and "disease". The clinicians must also evaluate the result from the knowledge of biological variation and be aware of the potential risk of false interpretation. Likewise, influence of random error and systematic errors on the result is of importance as well as the diagnostic sensitivity and specificity. The laboratory has certainly also a role and a responsibility in providing clinicians with adequate information that can assist them in the correct interpretation of the data. Clinical laboratory test

What is lab result mean?

Lab test results may be positive, negative, or inconclusive. Your doctor will discuss what your test results mean for you and your health.

A positive test result means that the substance or condition being tested for was found. Positive test results also can mean that the amount of a substance being tested for is higher or lower than normal.

A negative test results means that the substance or condition being tested for was not found. Negative results can also mean that the substance being tested for was present in a normal amount.

Inconclusive test results are those that are not clearly positive. For example, some tests measure the level of antibodies to some bacteria or viruses in blood or other fluid to look for an infection. It is not always clear if the level of antibodies is high enough to indicate an infection.

What are false-positive and false-negative test results?

A false-positive test result is one that shows a disease or condition is present when it is not present. A false-positive test result may suggest that a person has the disease or condition when he or she does not have it.

For example, a false-positive pregnancy test result would appear to detect the substance that confirms pregnancy, when in reality the woman is not pregnant.

A false-negative test result is one that does not detect what is being tested for even though it is present. A false-negative test result may suggest that a person does not have a disease or condition being tested for when he or she does have it.

For example, a false-negative pregnancy test result would be one that does not detect the substance that confirms pregnancy, when the women really are pregnant.

What if your results are different than the reference range?

> It is possible that is different than the reference range even though nothing is wrong with you.

> Sometimes certain factors can affect your test results, such as:

> Pregnancy
>
> Medicine you are taking
>
> Eating right before a test
>
> Smoking
>
> Being under stress

Why do values or reference ranges vary from lab to lab?

- Labs may use different types of equipment and tests, and sometimes they set their own reference ranges.
- Your lab report will contain the reference ranges your lab uses. Do not compare results from different labs.

Complete blood Count:

The CBC (with or without differential) is one of the most common blood tests.

The CBC can help detect blood diseases and disorders, such as anaemia, infections, clotting problems, blood cancers and immune system disorders.

Peripheral venous blood is collected in a lavender tube (contains the anticoagulant EDTA) and should be thoroughly mixed

Unacceptable specimen: Clotted or greater than 48 hours old

Methodology of testing: Whole blood analyzer Completed Blood Count

Red Blood Cells SI unit (normal value):

Male 4.3-5.9*106/mL

Female 3.5-5.0*106/mL

Deficiency of RBC:

1. Hemolytic anemia: decrease no of RBC

2. Excess bleeding

3. Hereditary spherocytosis: rare blood disorder in which defects in the red blood cells cause them to be shaped like spheres and break down easily.

Elevation of RBC:

1. Polycythaemia: Over production of RBC Primary polycythaemia: caused by overproduction of red blood cells by the bone marrow due to mutation or biological factor in the body.

2. Secondary polycythaemia: which is caused by factors that reduce the amount of oxygen reaching the body's tissues, such as smoking, high altitude or congenital heart disease. The red blood cells in some patients with secondary polycythemia may carry an abnormal form of haemoglobin that does not release oxygen readily (high-affinity haemoglobin).

Red blood cell enzyme disorders: Red blood cell enzyme disorders are important to recognize and diagnose for proper supportive care, monitoring, and treatment.

Glucose-6-phosphate dehydrogenase (G6PD) deficiency is an X- linked disorder most commonly characterized by episodic haemolysis in the setting of oxidative triggers, such as fava beans, infections, and certain medications.

Enzymopathies, such as pyruvate kinase deficiency, should be suspected in patients of all ages with a chronic haemolytic anaemia in the absence of immune-mediated haemolysis, a haemoglobinopathy, or evidence of a red cell membrane disorder.

Splenectomy partially ameliorates the anaemia in most patients with

Pyruvate kinase deficiency and other red blood cell enzyme disorders.

Glycolytic red cell disorders cause congenital haemolytic anaemias with wide clinical heterogeneity and frequent complications, including neonatal jaundice, gallstones, and both transfusion-related and transfusion- independent iron loading.

Mean Corpuscular Volume (MCV): MCV is a measure of the average size of your RBC. Abnormal MCV levels may be a sign of anaemia or thalassemia. Normal value: 76-100 mm3 Macrocytic: increase RBC size Microcytic: decrease RBC size

White Blood Cells

SI unit (normal value): 4000–11000/μL

Neutrophils: 2500-7500/μL

Eosinophil's: 500/μL

Basophils: 0-300/μL

Lymphocytes: 3000/μL

Monocytes: 200-600/ μL

Deficiency of WBC:

1. **Leukopenia:** decrease no of WBC

2. **Neutropenia:** decrease no of neutrophils (aplastic anaemia, chemotherapy, myelodysplasia, typhoid fever, hyperglycaemia)

3. **Basopenia:** decrease no of basophils (thyrotoxicosis, acute hypersensitivity reactions)

4. **Lymphocytopenia:** decrease no of lymphocytes (viral infection, systemic lupus erythematosus (SLS), rheumatoid arthritis, myasthenia gravis)

5. **Monocytopenia:** decrease no of monocytes (MonoMac Syndrome (the risk of infection with certain organisms, including a group of bacteria known as Mycobacterium avium complex (MAC) that are related to tuberculosis, human papillomavirus (HPV), and certain fungi.

Elevation in WBC:

1. **Leucocytosis:** increase no of WBC (>11000/µL)

2. **Neutrophilic leucocytosis:** increase no of neutrophils

3. **Basophilia:** increase no of basophils (hypothyroidism, myeloproliferative disorders) Eosinophilia: increase no of eosinophils (parasitic and fungal disease, allergies, skin disorders, toxins)

4. **Lymphocytic leucocytosis:** increase of lymphocytes

5. **Monocytosis:** increase no of monocytes (sarcoidosis, and Langerhans cell histiocytosis, autoimmune disorder)

Platelets

SI unit (normal value): 150000-450000/µL

Deficiency of Platelets: Thrombocytopenia: low number of platelets

Elevation in Platelets: Thrombocytosis: increase number of platelets (acute bleeding and blood loss, cancer, infections, removal of spleen.

Blood clotting test:

Factor V assay: This test measures Factor V, a substance involved in clotting. An abnormally low level may be indicative of liver disease, primary fibrinolysis (a breakdown of clots), or disseminated intravascular coagulation (DIC).

Fibrinogen level Fibrinogen is a protein made by your liver. This test measures how much fibrinogen is in your blood. Abnormal results may be a sign of excessive bleeding or haemorrhage, fibrinolysis, or placental abruption, which is a separation of the placenta from the uterine wall.

Prothrombin time (PT or PT-INR)

Prothrombin is another protein your liver produces. The prothrombin time (PT) test measures how well and how long it takes your blood to clot. It normally takes about 25 to 30 seconds. It may take longer if you take blood thinners. Other reasons for abnormal results include hemophilia, liver disease, and malabsorption. It's also useful in monitoring those who take medications that affect clotting, such as warfarin (Coumadin).

Typical reference ranges for healthy adults are:

Blood clotting test Time/ concentration

PT 9.0-11.7 sec

INR (coumadin) 0.9-1.2 sec

PTT (Heparin monitoring) 55.0-75.0 sec

APTT (therapeutic) 23.3-31.9 sec

Fibrinogen 203-377 mg/dl

Haemoglobin

SI unit (normal value) : Male 14–18 g/dL

Female 12–16 g/dL

Normocytic: haemoglobin levels are decrease but RBC size is normal (acute blood loss, anemia of chronic disease.

Microcytic: insufficiency of haemoglobin synthesis (iron deficiency of anemia, thalassemia)

Macrocytic: deficiency of vitamin B1 or folic acid (hypothyroidism, alcoholism) Sickle cell anaemia: alteration in haemoglobin structure

Hematocrit: Hematocrit is a measure how much space red blood cells take up in your blood. A high hematocrit level might mean dehydrated. A low hematocrit level might mean have anemia. Abnormal hematocrit levels also may be a sign of a blood or bone marrow disorder.

Laboratory test for Cardiac vascular system

Troponin: when muscle or heart cells are injured, troponin leaks out, and its level in blood is rise. Blood level of troponin rise when you have heart attack.

Ischemia modified albumin (IMA): high level of IMA indicates ischemia.

B-type natriuretic peptide test: natriuretic peptide (NP) test is a blood test that measures levels of a protein called BPN that is made by your heart and blood vessels. NP levels are higher than normal when you have heart failure.

Normal value : 100 (pg/mL)

Creatine Kinase (CK): diagnosis for acute MI, elevated level of CK diagnose myocardial infraction.

Normal value : <150 units/L

C-reactive protein (CRP): CRP is a marker for inflammation, and atherosclerosis has an inflammatory component. Patients with elevated levels of CRP have an increased risk for heart attack, stroke, sudden death, and vascular disease.

CRP levels less than 1: lower risk

CRP levels of 1 to 3: intermediate risk

CRP greater than 3: highest risk

Lipoprotein phospholipase A2 (Lp-PLA2): Elevations in the levels of Lp-PLA2 indicate greater risk of plaque formation and greater risk of cardiac events.

Measurement of total cholesterol:

A lipoprotein panel is a blood test that can help show whether you are at risk for coronary heart disease (CHD). This test looks at substances in your blood that carry cholesterol.

A lipoprotein panel gives information about your:

Total cholesterol

LDL ("bad") cholesterol. This is the main source of cholesterol buildup and blockages in the arteries.

HDL ("good") cholesterol. This type of cholesterol helps decrease blockages in the arteries.

Triglycerides- Triglycerides are a type of fat in your blood.

A lipoprotein panel measures the levels of LDL and HDL cholesterol and triglycerides in blood. Abnormal cholesterol and triglyceride levels may be signs of increased risk of CHD.

Most people will need to fast for 9 to 12 hours before a lipoprotein panel.

HDL cholesterol level HDL cholesterol category Less than 40 mg/dL A major risk factor for heart disease 40-59 mg/dL the higher, the better 60 mg/dL and above Considered protective against heart disease.

Triglyceride level

Triglyceride cholesterol category Less than 150mg/dL

Optimal 150-199 mg/dL

Borderline high 200-499 mg/dL

High 500 mg/dL Very high

Typical reference ranges for healthy adults are:

LDL cholesterol level LDL cholesterol category Less than 100mg/dL

Optimal 100-129 mg/dL

Near optimal / above optimal 130-159 mg/dL

Borderline high 160-189 mg/dL

High 190 mg/dL and above

Very high Lipoprotein Panel: The table below shows ranges for total cholesterol, LDL ("bad") cholesterol, and HDL ("good") cholesterol levels after 9 to 12 hours fasting. High blood cholesterol is a risk factor for CHF.

Typical reference ranges for healthy adults are:

Total cholesterol level Total cholesterol category

Less than 200mg/dL

Desirable 200-229 mg/dL

Borderline high 240 mg/dL and above High

Heart function test

Electrocardiogram (ECG): An ECG is a cardiac screening test that should be done on everyone on their first visit to a cardiologist. An EKG establishes baseline information about the structure of heart, its electrical conduction patterns and possible arrhythmias.

Echocardiogram: An echocardiogram is a noninvasive ultrasound cardiac screening test that records specific geographical areas of the beating heart, which reveals blood flow patterns and allows us to measure size and wall thickness of the heart's chambers.

Exercise/ Nuclear stress test: An exercise stress heart test is ordered to assess how heart is functioning when heart rate and blood pressure are increased during physical exertion.

Holter monitoring: A holter monitor is usually worn 24 hours and record every heart beat for that time period. Electrodes are placed on the chest, and a recorder is worn on a shoulder strap or belt. It is ordered to identify cardiac arrhythmias, and to monitor how well medication is working to minimize them.

Laboratory test for Liver

This group of tests indirectly assesses the health of liver cells by measuring enzymes arising from the cells and also assesses substances produced by the liver and used elsewhere in the body. If the liver enzymes are raised it can suggest damage to liver cells such as occurs with chronic alcoholism or with certain viral infections such as viral hepatitis. Some common liver function test include:

Alanine Transaminase test (ALT) ALT is used by our body to metabolize protein. If the liver is damaged or not functioning properly, ALT is released into the blood. This causes ALT levels to increase. A high result on this test can be a sign of liver damage.

Aspartate Transaminase test (AST) AST is an enzyme found in several parts of our body. Since AST levels aren't specific for liver damage, it's usually measured together with ALT to check for liver problems, when the liver is damaged, AST is released into the bloodstream. A high result on an AST test might indicate a problem with the liver or muscles.

Alkaline Phosphatase test (ALP) An ALP test is typically ordered in combination with several other tests. High levels of ALP may indicate liver damage, blockage of the bile ducts, or a bone disease.

Albumin test Albumin is the main protein made by your liver. An albumin test measure how well your liver is smoking this particular protein. A low result on this test indicates that your liver isn't functioning properly.

Bilirubin test Bilirubin is a waste product ordinarily processed by the liver. A damaged liver can't properly process bilirubin. This leads to an abnormally high level of bilirubin in the blood. A high result on the bilirubin test indicates that the liver isn't functioning properly.

Typical reference ranges for healthy adults are:

Lab result:

Normal value Comment AST 0-35 units/L with MI and liver injury

ALT 0-35 units/L negligibly unless parenchymal liver disease.

ALP 30-12- units/L in the bile duct obstruction, obstructive liver disease

CGT 0-70 units/L Sensitive test reflecting hepatocellular injury, usually in chronic alcoholics Bilirubin (total) 0.1-1 mg/dL

Breakdown product of haemoglobin, bound to albumin, conjugated in liver with hemolysis, cholestasis, liver injury

Laboratory test for Kidney

Urea clearance test: the urea clearance test requires a blood sample to measure the amount of urea in the blood stream and two urine specimens, collected one hour apart, to determine the amount of urea that is filtered, or cleared, by the kidneys into the urine.

Urine osmolality test: Urine osmolality is a measurement of the number of dissolved particles in urine. The test may be done on a urine sample collected first thing in the morning, on multiple time samples, or on a cumulative sample collected over a 24-hour period.

Blood urea nitrogen test (BUN): the BUN test measures the amount of nitrogen contained in the urea. High BUN levels can indicate kidney dysfunction, but because BUN is also affected by protein intake and liver function, the test is usually done together with a blood creatinine, a more specific indicator of kidney function.

Creatinine clearance test: With normal kidney function, the amount of creatinine in the blood remains relatively constant and normal. For this reason, and because creatinine is affected very little by liver function, an elevated blood creatinine level is a more sensitive indicator of impaired kidney function than the BUN.

Urine albumin: Healthy kidneys have filters (nephrons). These remove wastes but keep in large cells, like red blood cells and proteins. Albumin is one type of protein. When the filters are damaged, they may leak protein into your urine. Albumin levels can go up if you exercise a lot or have high blood sugar, too. Bladder infections can also make the levels go up.

Other blood test: Measurement of the blood levels of other elements regulated in part by the kidneys can also be useful in evaluating kidney function. These include sodium, potassium, carbon di oxide bicarbonate, calcium, magnesium, phosphorous, protein, uric acid and glucose. **Typical reference ranges for healthy adults are:**

Lab test SI unit (normal value) **Comment Sodium** 35-145 mmol/L usually caused by excess water (e.g., serum antidiuretic hormone) and is treated with water restriction. in severe dehydration, diabetes insipidus, significant renal and GI losses.

Potassium 3.5-5 mmol/L with renal dysfunction, acidosis, K-sparing diuretics, hemolysis, burn, crush, injuries by diuretics, or with alkaloids, severe vomiting and diarrhea.

CO2 22-28 mmol/L Sum of HCO3 and dissolved CO2. Reflects acid-base balance and compensatory pulmonary (CO2) and renal (HCO3-)

Calcium 8.5-10.5 mg/dL with hyperparathyroidism, paget disease, bone tumor, increased absorption from bone to ECF, decrease neuromuscular activity with dietary deficiency, increased excretion, pancreatitis, hypoparathyroidism, rickets, osteomalacia, renal insufficiency.

Chloride 98-106 mEq/L dehydration, multiple myeloma, kidney disorders, adrenal gland function

Phosphorus 2.4-4.1 mg/dL kidney and parathyroid gland dysfunction

Serum creatinine Women 0.6-1.1 mg/dL Men 0.7-1.3 mg/dL Creatinine clearance Women 88-128 mL/min Men 97-137 mL/min

Urine albumin 0-8 mg/dL

BUN 7-20 mg/dL

Urine microalbumin <30 mg (30-300 mg may mean early CKD, more than 300 mg may mean a later stage CKD

Albumin to Creatinine ratio <30 mg/gram

Laboratory test for Diabetes This table shows the ranges for blood glucose levels after 8 to 12 fasting (not eating). It shows the normal range and the normal ranges are a sign of prediabetes or diabetes. Diabetes Typical reference ranges for healthy adults are:

Plasma Glucose results (mg/dL) Diagnosis 70-99 Normal 100-125 Prediabetes 126 and above

Oral glucose tolerance test (OGTT) A two-hour, 75-gram oral glucose tolerance test (OGTT) is used to test for diabetes. A healthcare provider will take a fasting lab draw of blood to test your fasting glucose level first. They'll then ask you to drink 8 ounces of a syrupy glucose solution that contains 75 grams of sugar. You'll then wait in the office for two hours. The healthcare provider will draw blood at the one- and two-hour marks. Typical reference ranges for healthy adults are: When blood is drawn for prediabetes for diabetes for gestational diabetes

Fasting 100–125 mg/dL 126 mg/dL or greater than 92 mg/dL

After 1 hour greater than 180 mg/dL

After 2 hours 140–199 mg/dL 200 mg/dL or greater than 153 mg/dL

Haemoglobin A1c (HbA1c) The haemoglobin A1c test tells you your average level of blood sugar over the past 2 to 3 months. It's also called HbA1c, glycated haemoglobin test, and glycohemoglobin. People who have diabetes need this test regularly to see if their levels are staying within range. It can tell if you need to adjust your diabetes medicines. The A1c test is also used to diagnose diabetes. When glucose builds up in your blood, it binds to the haemoglobin in your red blood cells. The A1c test measures how much glucose is bound.

HbA1c & Average Blood Glucose Levels

	A1C Percentage	Average Blood Glucose Levels	
Normal	<5.7%	<117 mg/dL	6.5 mmol/L
Prediabetes	5.7–6.4%	117–137 mg/dL	6.5–7.6 mmol/L
Diabetes	>6.4%	> 137 mg/dL	> 7.6 mmol/L
	6.5%	140 mg/dL	7.8 mmol/L
	7.0%	154 mg/dL	8.6 mmol/L
	7.5%	169 mg/dL	9.4 mmol/L
	8.0%	183 mg/dL	10.1 mmol/L
	8.5%	197 mg/dL	10.9 mmol/L
	9.0%	212 mg/dL	11.8 mmol/L
	9.5%	226 mg/dL	12.6 mmol/L
	10%	240 mg/dL	13.4 mmol/L

Increased risk of complications

Thyroid function tests: This group of tests assesses the thyroid gland which regulates metabolism in the body. The whole group will be ordered f there are signs of low or high thyroid hormone output on physical examination. Sometimes just one test-the TSH will be ordered to rule out a thyroid problem when symptoms might be difficult to explain.

The usual blood tests done for thyroid function are TSH, T4 and sometimes T3. usually the 'free' or active portion of T4 and T3 is measured (i.e., FT4 and FT3). Laboratories use reference ranges to compare blood test results with results in the normal healthy population. Typical reference ranges for healthy adults are:

Test Normal values

TSH 0.4-4.0 mU/L

FT4 9.0-25.0 pmol/L

FT3 3.5-7.8 pmol/L

Vitamin D Normal range: 30 to 74 ng/mL

25-hydroxy vitamin D: When calcium is low and/or a person has symptoms of vitamin D deficiency, such as bone malformation in children (rickets) and bone weakness, softness, or fracture in adults (osteomalacia), 25-hydroxyvitamin D usually is ordered to identify a possible deficiency in vitamin D.

1,25-dihydroxyvitamin D This testing may be ordered when kidney disease or abnormalities of the enzyme that converts 25-hydroxyvitamin D to 1,25-dihydroxyvitamin D is suspected. Rarely, this test may be done when calcium is high or a person has a disease that might produce excess amounts of vitamin D, such as sarcoidosis or some forms of lymphoma (because immune cells may make 1,25-dihydroxyvitamin D).

Vitamin B12 Normal Values

Infants up to age 6 months: 0.4 mcg

Babies age 7-12 months: 0.5 mcg

Children age 1-3 years: 0.9 mcg

Kids age 4-8 years: 1.2 mcg

Children age 9-13 years: 1.8 mcg

Teens age 14-18: 2.4 mcg (2.6 mcg per day if pregnant and 2.8 mcg per day if breastfeeding)

Adults: 2.4 mcg (2.6 mcg per day if pregnant and 2.8 mcg per day if breastfeeding)

Deficiency of B12

Atrophic gastritis, in which stomach lining has thinned

Pernicious anemia, which makes it hard for your body to absorb vitamin B12

Conditions that affect your small intestine, such as Crohn's disease, celiac disease, bacterial growth, or a parasite

Immune system disorders, such as Graves' disease or lupus

Laboratory Tests for Lung Infections

Blood tests or cultures.

Blood tests may help tell whether antibodies to a specific organism that can cause pneumonia are present or whether specific viruses, such as influenza (flu) or respiratory syncytial virus (RSV), are present. Doctors can use blood cultures to test for bacteria in your bloodstream.

Oximetry: An oximeter can estimate the amount of oxygen in your blood. A sensor in a cuff or clip is placed on the end of your finger. This sensor measures how much oxygen is in your blood. The oximeter machine shows the result.

Arterial blood gases: An arterial blood gas test can measure the levels of oxygen in a sample of blood drawn from your artery. Doctors use this test to find out whether enough oxygen is getting into your bloodstream from your lungs.

Bronchoscopy: Bronchoscopy is a visual examination of the tubes leading to your lungs. This test is usually done by a respirologist (lung specialist). He or she inserts a small, lighted device through your nose or mouth into the tubes leading to your lungs. During the procedure, the doctor can obtain samples of tissue, fluid, or mucus. Laboratory tests for lung infections

Transtracheal mucus cultures (rarely done): Transtracheal sputum cultures are tests performed on a mucus sample obtained directly from your windpipe (trachea).

Lung biopsy: A lung biopsy is a test done on a very small piece of lung tissue to look for conditions such as lung cancer or fibrous tissue in the lungs (pulmonary fibrosis). Your doctor obtains lung tissue by inserting a needle into your chest between two ribs or by using bronchoscopy.

Thoracentesis: Thoracentesis involves puncturing the chest wall to obtain fluid from the space around the lungs. Fluid obtained during the test can be checked for signs of infection or cancer.

Computed tomography (CT) scan: A CT scan uses X-rays to produce detailed pictures of structures inside your body. It may be used in people who are not responding to their treatment.

Other blood test

Blood test for infection Antibodies and sometimes antigens can be measured for other infecting agents. The commonly performed tests include:

Epstein Barr virus

Toxoplasmosis

Cytomegalovirus

Streptococcal bacteria

Leptospirosis

Rubella Virus

It requires caution interpreting these test results because the antibody tests may often indicate past infection-not current infection.

Blood Culture Test- this is usually carried out as an urgent test in cases of serious infection where the doctor suspects that a bacteria is multiplying with in the blood stream.

Blood Test Commonly Ordered Singly

Serum Amylase- this is commonly ordered in cases of abdominal pain to see if the pancrease gland is inflamed or its duct obstructed.

Follicle stimulating hormone (FSH)- Sustained high levels of FSH in a women can indicate that the menopause is approaching or has happened. Normal level: 5-20 mIU/ml

Progesterone level – progesterone measurements are often used to determine if ovulation has occurred. The ovaries produce very small amounts of progesterone until ovulation happens. Normal level- 3ng/mL

Beta Human Chronic Gonadotropin (HCG)- this is the hormone produced in early pregnancy and is the basis of the urine pregnancy tests. An HCG level of less than 5 mIU/mL is considered negative for pregnancy, and anything above 25 mIU/mL is considered positive for pregnancy.

DHEA-S or dehydroepiandrosterone- is another male hormone that is found in all women. DHEA-S is an androgen that is secreted by the adrenal gland. It is normal for women to have DHEA-S levels anywhere between 35-430 ug/dl. Most women with PCOS tend to have DHEA-S levels greater than 200 ug/dl.

Prolactin - is a pituitary hormone that stimulates and sustains milk production in nursing mothers. Prolactin levels are usually normal in women with PCOS, generally less than 25 ng/ml. However, it is important to check for high prolactin levels in order to rule out other problems, such as a pituitary tumor, that might be causing PCOS-related symptoms. Some women with PCOS do have elevated prolactin levels, typically falling within the 25-40 ng/ml range.

Autoimmune Disease test

Autoimmune disease are a group of disease where the body's immune system incorrectly interprets certain of its own tissues as a foreign invader and produces an immune response to attack hat tissue. The best-known autoimmune disease is rheumatoid arthritis where the immune system attacks the slippery lubricated lining inside certain joints. The blood test tries to measure specific antibodies produces by the body against specific tissues.

Such tests include:

    Rheumatoid factor

    Lupus anticoagulant test

    Antinuclear antibody test

    The ESR test (erythrocyte sedimentation rate) is a rate on red cells but is included here as it is often used to monitor the response of autoimmune diseases to treatment. If raised it any be a general pointer to an infective or inflammatory process going on in the body.

Drug Assays

The level of certain drugs can be measured in the serum. The commonly performed drug assays are usually those where the drug has a fine line between being toxic and therapeutic.

The common assays include:

Serum digoxin

Serum phenytoin

Serum theophylline

Serum lithium

Serum alcohol

Serum lipids

Some other common tests

Disease Marker Test: Blood tests can monitor the levels of certain chemicals in the blood as an indicator of the progress of a disease.

The best known of these tests is the PSA (prostate specific antigen) test which is monitored in prostate cancer.

The AFP (alpha foeto-protein) is another-used for monitoring treatment for liver cancer.

Ca-125, is used to monitor progress in ovarian cancer.

Tissue histology: FNA = Fine needle aspiration- A fine needle on a syringe is inserted into a lesion and negative pressure is applied to suck up some cells for microscopy. This is usually to check for tumor cells. Excision Biopsy- this is where an entire lesion is removed and sliced up into thin sections for microscopy.

Biopsy- this is where a small part of a lesion is removed for microscopy to try and make a diagnosis

Microbiology- any moist area on the body can be swabbed with a sterile cotton tipped bud, plated out on to agar jelly plates and placed into an incubator to see if bacteria will grow from swab. Once the bacteria have grown, they can be identified under the microscope and tested to for sensitivity test (C& S). Scrapings of tissue or cuttings of nails can be similarly treated for fungal lesions.

- If there is a delay between taking the swab and plating it out, it has to store in special transport media.
- Sputum is commonly cultured for bacteria causing bronchitis, pneumonia and tuberculosis. Faeces can be cultured for bacterial, viral and parasitic organisms.

Cytology- Cytology involves obtaining a normal tissue fluid and examining it under the microscope for early signs of cancer cells.

Sexually Transmitted Disease (STD) Blood Tests

VDRL/TPHA- these are screening tests for syphilis.

HIV- this is a screening test for the presence of Human Immunodeficiency Virus antibody. **Herpes antibodies-** can be measured to assess past or present herpes simplex infection.

Hepatitis antibody- and antigen testing can be included in the STD tests as well as with Liver Function Tests. The various types of hepatitis can be contracted by other means as well as sexual transmission however.